THE
SCANDINAVIAN
WORLD

THE
SCANDINAVIAN
WORLD

Arland O. Fiske

North American Heritage Press
Minot, North Dakota

THE SCANDINAVIAN WORLD

International Standard Book Number: 0-942323-02-5

Library of Congress Catalog Number: 87-60604

Published by
North American Heritage Press
A DIVISION OF
CREATIVE MEDIA, INC.
P.O. Box 1
Minot, North Dakota 58702
701/852-5552

Printed in the United States of America

Dedication

To

Paul

Michael

Lisa

Daniel

Mark

John

Christopher

Our "Scandinavian Heritage"

CONTENTS

THE SCANDINAVIAN WORLD

FOREWORD

WHEN IN 1980 ARLAND FISKE began writing short bits of history and legend about Scandinavia, he may not have realized that the enterprise would capture him. Now, 300 episodes later, he has published his second collection of these stories that have appeared separately in newspapers throughout our country.

One wonders how a busy parish pastor could have found the time and energy for this hobby which must have taken hundreds of hours of "bloodhound" research. He was pursuing the roots of his own family's Danish-Finnish-Norwegian-Swedish heritage, of course. Whatever else has driven him to do it, he has given to us all a charming overview of these lands, their people, and their large immigrant family in our country.

The book will be of special interest to people of Scandinavian roots, but Fiske's gift of imagination and facile pen makes the book fascinating for anyone who loves human interest literature.

One look at the table of contents will capture you. You will want your friends to have the book too.

—Alvin N. Rogness
President Emeritus
Luther Northwestern Theological Seminary
St. Paul, Minnesota

PREFACE

THE MORE I LEARN about the heritage of the Scandinavian world, the more in debt I become to a host of people, the vast majority who are unknown to me except for what has been written by them or about them. The heritage includes love of life and freedom, religious faith, stories of heroism and sacrifice, and a legacy which makes one both humble and proud. The Scandinavian world, of course, goes far beyond those lands of the North Atlantic. Many of us who have been transplanted to the New World continue to have strong emotional ties with these lands and their people.

Some people may wonder if the world would have known the difference if those lands of the North had remained frozen in the Ice Age or their people had never existed at all. Their total population is less than 25 million in a world which exceeds five billion. Even if you add another 25 million or more who acknowledge having Scandinavian blood in the rest of the world, it remains a small number.

However, when looked at from the "inside," as I have for over 60 years, it's quite another story. I see myself mirrored in the lives of these Norsemen of past generations, including my parents, grandparents and the countless numbers who lived before them.

Some of the heritage requires humor and some absolution. Maybe that's why Norwegians in particular enjoy telling ethnic jokes about themselves. But other records from the past bring excitement and even tears of gratitude for those little known people who have been described in the literature that is a part of the heritage. Even in the New World — several generations removed from the lands of our origins — we're drawn together by the story of our forebears and the land they left in search of a better life elsewhere.

My family has encouraged me to record for them some of the stories that reflect their heritage so they can share in its treasures. I'm grateful to them for prodding me on, even when I was busy in my profession of ministry and theology to continue this interesting hobby. Chapter 61, "The Anatomy of a Story," tells the reader how this project came into being.

I'm also grateful to the many people with whom I've visited in shopping malls, who have written letters, called me on the telephone or stopped in to express their appreciation for the stories previously published. Many people have added to my files of information by sharing family histories and other anecdotes. It has been a generous reward for this work of love to have discovered so many new friends. I also welcome their corrections to anything about which I was misinformed or inadequately informed.

There's a reason why the stories in the beginning of the book are shorter than those near the end. It all has to do with the space available when they were originally printed in a local newspaper. When the Minot Daily News purchased the Area Market Review and requested to continue the column, more space became available. The articles, of course, have been re-edited for publication in book form.

Besides my wife, Gerda, whose name comes from a beautiful Norse goddess, our children also continue to find pride in their heritage. I owe a special debt to all the friends with whom I have worked for ten years in putting on the Norsk Høstfest each October since 1978. I am deeply indebted to Allen O. Larson and the North American Heritage Press for making this book possible. Thanks to Tammy Wolf for preparing the manuscript for publication; to Sheldon Larson for designing the cover; and to my daughter, Lisa Gaylor, who combines motherhood with her profession as an artist, and who has done the illustrations. Thanks to all the readers who follow the "Scandinavian Heritage" column and who make this publication a success by purchasing the books, "The Scandinavian Heritage" (1987) and this new volume, "The Scandinavian World." Additional titles are being planned.

While I intend this book to be informative and even inspirational for everyone, I hope that my Swedish friends will find some special delight in it as they celebrate 350 years in America during 1988. Welcome to the "Scandinavian World" and happy reading to all!

— Arland O. Fiske, Minot, North Dakota
  June 6, 1988, Swedish Flag Day

CHAPTER 1

The Swedes
Of Jamestown, New York

MY FRIEND, PAUL SETTERGREN, stopped by for a visit before he moved to Jamestown, New York. He brought a book for me to read, entitled "Saga From the Hills: A History of the Swedes of Jamestown." Its 700 pages offers insight on all Swedes who came to America.

Sweden was generous to the New World. 1,200,000 Swedes (25% of the population) came to America. The earliest Swedish communities began on the Delaware river in the 1638. They were not, however, allowed to live in peace. The Dutch and then the English grabbed their territory and they did not continue to expand as a Swedish colony.

Two hundred years later, starting in the 1840s, when the large movement of immigrants were arriving, the Swedes were determined to remember their culture and heritage. They started coming to Jamestown in 1850. Wilton E. Bergstrand offered fives reasons for this choice: 1) the natural beauty; 2) healthful climate; 3) fresh water; 4) valuable forests; 5) good farmland.

But why did they leave their homeland? First, the upper classes (nobility, gentry and government officials) had most of the privileges. In America, they could vote. Second, military duty was required for men at age 19 and Sweden had been involved in many continental wars. But they weren't cowards. More than 3000 immigrants from Sweden fought to free the slaves in America's Civil War. Third, many wanted to get away from the state church system. Though there were many faithful and effective clergy, the men of the cloth were seen as a class aligned with the nobility and as opposed to social change. While the immigrants loved their native land, America meant a new start for them in a world of freedom and opportunity.

The Swedes were welcome in Jamestown because they brought needed skills in wood and metal working. Soon they became executives and owners of businesses. They also had a reputation for great physical

1

strength. One Swedish immigrant bought a stove, had it strapped on his back and carried the 250 pound load to his house on top of Swede Hill.

I asked Settergren (himself a Swede) how many Swedish people live in the Jamestown area. He estimated about 35,000. That rivals Rockford, Illinois, another strong Swedish-American community.

The Swedes were considered desirable settlers because they had a reputation for honesty. They were noted for being hard workers and having respect for the law. They were also strong community builders. Karl Peterson, one of the Jamestown settlers, invented the Crescent line of tools.

Christian faith was important to Swedish immigrants. They built over 2000 churches in America, the largest being First Lutheran in Jamestown. One Swedish farmer near Jamestown came to pay his bill at the store after harvest and was asked by the storekeeper if he wanted a receipt. "No, God knows I have paid my bill," he replied. The storekeeper sneered, "Do you still believe in God?" Confessing to be a believer, he asked: "Don't you?" When the storekeeper replied "Naw!" the farmer said, "Then you better give me a receipt." He wasn't taking chances.

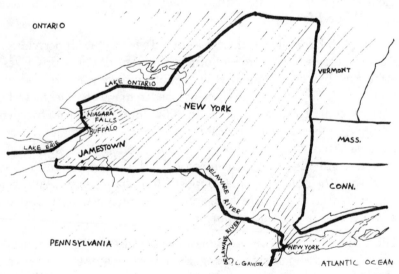

Early Swedish-American settlements.

CHAPTER 2

Gutzon Borglum —
Sculptor Of Presidents

WHEN THE WAR BETWEEN THE STATES was over, immigration to the New World began with gusto. Among those who came to America was the Borglum family from Denmark. James Borglum, a classics scholar and medical student, being angry over the way his family's estate was divided, took his young wife to the border of Utah and Idaho. There Gutzon was born on March 25, 1867. One day, while still too small to understand, he remembered his mother giving him a goodbye kiss and walking out the door never to return.

Gutzon's father remarried and moved to St. Louis to complete his medical degree. From there they moved to Fremont and later to Omaha, Nebraska. Gutzon had bad feelings towards his stepmother and so he went off to a boarding school in St. Mary's, Kansas. While there, he fell in love with art. This displeased his parents, but being made of the same stubborn qualities as his father, he persisted. Their move to Los Angeles when he was 17 gave him the chance he wanted.

His special love was horses. One of his paintings, called "Staging in California," pictured a stage coach with runaway horses flying along a mountain cliff. This caught the attention of General John Fremont, famed for his exploration of the "Oregon Trail." His career was launched when he painted the general's portrait. In 1890, Gutzon, with his new bride, went to study art in Paris.

The United Daughters of the Confederacy commissioned Borglum to carve a 20 foot head of General Lee on Stone Mountain in Georgia. He was also to have done General "Stonewall" Jackson and Jefferson Davis, president of the Confederacy. His patrons, however, tried to cheat him and so he destroyed the plans. Then they tried to have him arrested, but he escaped across the state line and was given asylum by the governor. However, if you ever go to Atlanta, take a drive out to Stone Mountain. The work was completed by another artist in 1916. A dazzling

3

laser show is held by the carvings after dark.

Among his many statues were those of General Sheridan, the Wright Brothers airplane, James Smithson (Smithsonian Institute), the Gettysburg Memorial, which President Wilson commissioned for Poland, and the remodelling of the torch on the Statue of Liberty.

Borglum's most famous work was the presidents' heads at Mt. Rushmore in South Dakota. Begun in 1925, it was not completed until Oct. 31, 1941, seven months after the famed sculptor died. His son, Lincoln, finished the work. The final cost was $989,991.32, a fantastic bargain! It took so long because the project would run out of money and had to wait for congress to approve new funding. Denmark is proud of the Mt. Rushmore memorial. When I visited Legoland, near Vejle in Denmark, I saw a miniature Mt. Rushmore built out of Lego blocks.

While the work in the Black Hills was taking place, Borglum was in great demand elsewhere. A temperamental artist, it was not unusual for him to pick up an ax and smash what others thought to be a masterpiece. While doing the statue of a horse for the Sheridan Hotel in Chicago, he knocked off a leg, saying, "I'd rather be late in delivering it, than give Chicago something less than perfect."

Having experienced a painful childhood, Borglum was devoted to his family. His artistic tradition was carried on by his son, Lincoln, who completed his father's statue of Christ on a mountain overlooking Mt. Rushmore. His son added gentleness to the statue, picturing Christ as teacher giving the "Sermon on the Mount" and inviting all viewers to "come unto me." The next time you go to Mt. Rushmore, remember the son of the immigrant physician from Denmark who became America's most famous sculptor.

The presidents
at Mt. Rushmore.

CHAPTER 3

Sigurd
The Crusader

I T'S HARD TO FIND A MORE COLORFUL Scandinavian than Sigurd ("Jerusalemfarer"), son of King Magnus Barefoot. It was an exciting time to be a Christian ruler for those were the years of the Crusades to wrest the "Holy Land" from the hands of the "Infidels."

Sigurd shared the rule of Norway with his brother Eystein. They were only about 13 or 14 years old when coming into power. Eystein ruled the north and Sigurd the south. It was decided, however, that while Sigurd was off to wage the "holy war," Eystein should be in charge. It worked remarkably well.

Sailing with 60 ships in 1108, Sigurd first paid a visit to King Henry of England, the son of William the Conqueror, also of Norse descent. Sigurd's crusade does not seem to fit into any of the nine noted Crusades, but he did fight a series of battles with the "heathens" in Spain, Portugal and the islands on the way. (It is not correct to call Muslims "heathens" by today's definition, as they hold a monotheistic view of God. They also had a superior civilization to the Christians of western Europe.) According to Snorri Sturluson in his "Sagas of the Norse Kings," Sigurd's terms of peace were: "No man he spared who would not take the Christian faith for Jesus' sake." The people back home responded generously with gifts to support the cause. The crusades were profitable to the victors. Great amounts of booty were carried away in the Viking ships.

Sigurd stopped in Sicily to make Duke Roger into a king. Roger was one of the Norman rulers in Italy and Sicily. In Palestine, he was met by the Christian King Baldwin who spread valuable clothes on the road for the "red carpet" welcome into Jerusalem. Not only was Sigurd given a magnificent feast, but he was given a splinter of the "holy cross" on condition that he would promote Christianity with all his power, secure an archbishop for Norway and collect a tithe. The fragment of the cross

5

was to be placed by St. Olaf's body in Trondheim. This induced many more pilgrims to Trondheim to venerate St. Olaf's relics.

Jerusalem behind, Sigurd sailed for Constantinople to visit Emperor Kirialax. Again precious cloths were spread over the road to impress the visitors. Sigurd had the horses of his royal guard shod with golden shoes and gave instruction that one fall off in public view. They were to act as though nothing had happened. Upon leaving, he gave his fleet to the emperor and many of the Northmen joined the imperial guard. He made his way home across land, being entertained by Christian kings along the way. At age 23, he returned from three years of crusading, the most famous king of the North.

The Crusaders have left their mark in Palestine. I was impressed by the magnificent churches they built and by the ruins of the castles left behind from their 200 year period. The Lutheran Church in Jerusalem today worships in a Crusader building. When I worshipped there in 1985, the English service was led by Pastor Calvin Storley of Minneapolis who has Norwegian ancestry. Sigurd would have liked that.

The Crusaders were finally defeated by a Kurdish warrior named Saladin who re-captured Jerusalem for Islam in 1187. While motivated by pious intentions, the Crusades remain one of the greatest scandals in the history of the church. King Sigurd, however, became the most reknowned hero of the North. He died at age 40 and Snorri wrote that the "time of his reign was good for the country; for there was peace, and the crops were good."

CHAPTER 4

Carl Milles —
Swedish Artistic Genius

MY FIRST ENCOUNTER WITH CARL MILLES (1875-1955) was when we moved to St. Louis in 1961. I used to travel a good deal by railroad in those days. out in front of the old St. Louis Train Depot is a large set of sculptures called "Meeting of the Waters." It was finished by Milles in 1940.

It's a grandiose display of 14 bronze sculptures with water spouting and spraying. The fountains symbolize the coming together of the Missouri and Mississippi rivers just north of the city. Whenever I visit the home town of Cardinal baseball, I like to take another look at this famous work of art. It's located on Market Street about a half mile west of Busch Stadium and the famed Gateway Arch. Today the old train depot has been converted into a classy shopping mall, but Milles' work of art stands as grand as ever.

One of the questions that goes through my mind when I read of people who turn out to be winners is about their early years of life. How did they get started on the road to success? Milles was born near Uppsala, Sweden. It's an historic and cultural area of the country. At age 17, he became apprenticed to a cabinet maker in Stockholm and attended a technical school. Four years later Milles took off for Paris to study art under the famous Auguste Rodin, well known in the school of Impressionism. He remained in Paris for eight years.

Milles was so engrossed in his study of sculpturing that he got a lung inflammation from breathing stone dust. It bothered him for the rest of his life. By 1908 he was well enough to return to Sweden and settled in the suburb of Lidingo in Stockholm. There he built a studio called "Millesgarten."

In 1920, Milles became a professor at the Swedish Royal Academy. It wasn't long, however, before he found this too confining and returned to his studio. In 1931, he was invited to be the head of the department of sculpture at Cranbrook Academy of Art in Bloomfield Hills,

7

Michigan. Now he made his name in America as well as in Europe. In 1945, Milles became an American citizen and turned over the management of his beloved "Millesgarten" to a private institution. During the winters of 1950-55, he was at the American Academy in Rome. He died at the age of 80 in his native Sweden.

Two famous teachers left their mark on Milles: Rodin, the impressionist from Paris and the German sculptor-theorist, Adolf von Hildebrand, who helped him to blend classical art forms (Greek and Roman) with the Nordic goblins and trolls.

Milles, however, developed his own special style. He had a flair for charming decorative effects. Among his well known works are "Europa and the Bull" in Halmstad, Sweden. He did one of Sten Sture, a popular Swedish patriot. The "Folkunga Fountain" in Linkoping, Sweden, pictures a rider on a wild steed. There are 20 of his sculptures in Stockholm alone. That's how much the Swedes think of him.

I am not an artist or a student of art. But I've learned a lot from artists and my appreciation of them grows with years. If you go to St. Louis, be sure to see the "Meeting of the Waters" and remember Carl Milles, Sweden's artistic genius. Better still, go to Stockholm and see "Millesgarten." The Swedes will love you for just asking to visit their favorite sculptor's art treasures.

*Millesgarten
in Stockholm.*

CHAPTER 5

Raoul Wallenberg —
'Righteous Gentile'

RAOUL WALLENBERG IS THE MOST famous "missing person" in the world. There's a million dollar reward for his safe return to freedom. A few people know his fate, but most westerners don't believe their explanation.

The Wallenbergs are a respected Swedish family, distinguished as statesmen, diplomats and bankers. Raoul was born August 4, 1912, into a less wealthy branch of the family. His father, a naval officer, died three months before his birth. Fortunately, he had a strong hearted mother.

After graduating with distinction in architecture from the University of Michigan in 1935, Raoul tried banking in South Africa and Palestine. He found it to be "too calm, cynical and cold." Architecture was his dream, though he went into international trade. The family thought his talents were in politics.

While in Palestine, Wallenberg came in contact with Jewish refugees from Germany. He was moved by their persecution and by the anti-semitism which he found. It touched him more deeply because his great-great grandfather, Michael Benedicks, was a German Jew.

During World War II, the evidence was mounting that most European Jews were being destroyed by Hitler. Adolf Eichmann, a heartless sadist, came to Hungary in March 1944 to personally exterminate the country's Jewish population. His cunning and cruelty knew no bounds. The Allied powers were slow to respond with help. But finally, President Roosevelt gave his support to save them through the U.S. War Refugee Board.

Strange as it may seem, it finally came down to one man, 31 year old Raoul Wallenberg. He joined the Swedish legation in Budapest and assembled 250 Jewish volunteers who were given Swedish diplomatic protection. He rented 32 houses over which he flew the Swedish flag to shelter 15,000 Jews and set up two hospitals, soup kitchens and a children's home. Portuguese, Swiss and Vatican legations also gave help. Surviving many Nazi attempts to kill him, it is believed that he saved over 100,000 Jews of Budapest by giving them "protective passes." Bribery and threats of post-war punishment were his weapons against the Nazis.

On Jan. 17, 1945, as the Russian army approached, Wallenberg was summoned to the Soviet military headquarters. Though warned against going, he went in hopes of negotiating with them on behalf of the Jewish people. Soviet paranoia and treachery, however, regarded him as a danger to their rule. That was his last day of freedom.

Until late 1987, there was hope that Wallenberg was still alive. Then the Kremlin advised his family that he died of a heart attack in a Soviet prison in 1947. Despite this report which has been accepted by his family as factual, there are former Soviet prisoners who have returned to the West, and claimed they had seen him and spoken to him since that time.

The government of Israel has declared Wallenberg a "Righteous Gentile." The United States government has made him an "honorary citizen." He is only one of three foreign nationals ever to be granted such a recognition. As a part of the "New Sweden '88" celebration, Gustavus Adolphus College in St. Peter, Minnesota, had a special lecture on Wallenberg by Ambassador Per Anger who had been a personal friend and colleague of Wallenberg.

A tree has been planted in his honor at Yad Vashem, Israel's memorial to the Holocaust victims near Jerusalem. It was with deep emotion that I paused before that tree, silent in my heart for the Holocaust victims, but proud that a great Scandiavian had sacrificed his life in this mission of mercy.

CHAPTER 6

Norway Honors
General Jones

IN THE STUDENT UNION BUILDING of Minot State University, there is a room dedicated to the honor of General David C. Jones, United States Air Force. He was Chairman of the Joint Chiefs of Staff from 1978-1982, the highest military position of the United States. My friend, Ken Robertson, retired Air Force and Curator of the room's memorabilia, called my attention to Norway's recognition of the University's famous alumnus. He also supplied much of the information for this story.

On November 24, 1981, Gen. Jones was awarded the Grand Cross of the Royal Order of St. Olav, Norway's highest decoration for non-Norwegians in peacetime. The ceremony took place at the Norwegian Ambassador's residence in Washington, D.C. The presentation was made by Ambassador Knut Hedemann and Gen. Sverre Hamre, Norwegian Chief of Defense.

King Olav V of Norway honored Gen. Jones "in recognition of his outstanding military service as Chief of Staff for the United States Air Force, 1974-1978, and as Chairman of the Joint Chiefs of Staff since 1978."

The "Order of St. Olav" was established on Aug. 21, 1847, by King Oscar I, who was king of both Norway and Sweden. This recognition is an honor that Norway gives to a non-Norwegian. (The reader should understand that even ethnic Norwegians living in America are considered "non-Norwegians" in Norway.) The Order has three ranks: Grand Cross, Commander and Knight. The insignia has a golden cross with white enamel and a golden lion on a globe of red enamel in the center. On the reverse side is the motto: "Ret og Sandhed" ("Justice and Truth"). The King of Norway is the Order's Grand Master and all insignia are to be returned to him after the death of the recipient.

The award is given for "outstanding merit for the country or for humanity." Gen. Jones qualified for this recognition because Norway is a loyal and appreciative member of NATO. Sharing a common border with the Soviet Union, Norway could be a target for political blackmail without American support. The huge Soviet naval base at Murmansk is close to the nothern tip of Norway.

General Jones was born in Aberdeen, South Dakota, in 1921, and moved to Minot in 1930. After graduating from Minot High School in 1939, he attended both the University of North Dakota in Grand Forks and Minot State University. He had his first flying lessons in Minot in 1941 under the tutelage of Bill Gunn. Right after Pearl Harbor, in January 1942, he married Lois Tarbell, of Rugby, ND, who was teaching in a nearby rural school. Then he volunteered for the United States Army Air Force and reported to the Roswell, New Mexico, cadet school.

One of Lois' former pupils told me that the future Air Force General was an occasional visitor to the rural school. At recess time he played ball with the students. One day, he took a homerun swing and shattered their new Louisville Slugger bat. They have forgiven him, however, in the light of his later achievements. Besides that, they thought it was special that he'd play ball with them.

If you visit the Minot State University campus, be sure to look at the many recognitions which have been bestowed on North Dakota's famed general.

CHAPTER 7

The 'Ola And Per'
Comics

FROM 1918 TO 1935, PETER JULIUS ROSENDAHL (1878-1942), a farmer from Spring Grove, Minnesota, produced the comic series "Olga og Per" ("Ole and Peter"). It had a large readership, even though often produced only in the off-seasons.

The first paper to carry the series was the "Decorah-Posten," well known among Norwegian-American immigrant families. The cartoons were used to increase their subscription list. The paper reached a circulation of 45,000 during the 1920s, but dropped to 35,000 by 1950. In 1972, the subscription list was sold to the "Western Viking" in Seattle which continues to reprint them. When I asked my mother if she had read "Ola og Per," she gave an immediate recollection.

Born of Norwegian immigrant parents, Rosendahl also wrote poetry and song texts. Besides drawing cartoons, he painted portraits. He travelled very little and his only formal training was a correspondence course in cartooning from a school in Minneapolis. His father was from Hadeland, near Oslo, and his wife was a Halling. These places were also the backgrounds for the two main characters. Ola, the Halling, wore overalls and carried a pitchfork over his shoulder. Per, the Hadeling, appeared in a long-tailed suit and carried a big monkey wrench around the farm. In contrast to Ola who was short, stocky, sensible and hard working, Per was a tall and lanky dreamer.

The comic strip included Per's brother Lars. He was university educated, but absolutely useless on the farm. Having no idea how to harness a horse, he became the butt of community jokes. Polla, Ola's plump wife who came from Fargo, North Dakota, preferred city life and had no idea how to milk a cow. Her mother came out to the farm and turned out to be a real battle-axe.

These cartoons helped to popularize 'Norwegian stories." You can imagine the immigrants gathering in the small town cafe and roaring with laughter over such numbskull stories and riddles. After 1935, Rosendahl

13

refused to draw any more cartoons and in 1942 he took his own life.

The "Ola og Per" comics used a slapstick approach to picture Norwegian-American life. They were in the style of "Mutt and Jeff," the "Katzenjammer Kids" and "Bringing Up Father." The Norwegian dialects come through in the cartoons.

A new volume entitled "Han Ola og han Per" ("He's Ole and he's Peter") was printed both in Norwegian and in English. It contains the first 223 comic strips of the 599 that were published. Edited by Joan Buckley and Einar Haugen, it was published by the Norwegian-American Historical Association and the University Press in Oslo. One of the interesting features of the book is the vocabulary list at the bottom of each page. It's a good way to learn the folksy language of the immigrants, half filled with English.

These cartoons dealt with the struggles of immigrants in a strange land. The characters have both foibles and redeeming qualities. While many of the scenes were "violent," nobody ever got hurt. It's mostly reflexive humor, it turns back on the person who tries to be dramatic. We are indebted to the editors and publishers for making this fine volume available.

The people of Spring Grove still regard Rosendahl as one of their local heroes and a daughter-in-law, Georgia Rosendahl, is the local genealogist for the community.

CHAPTER 8

Halvdan
The Black

"HALVDAN THE BLACK" (820-860?) seems a strange name to our ears. Halvdan means "half Dane." His mother, Asa, was a Danish princess. His father descended from the royal Swedish family of Ynglings and was king of Vestfold in southern Norway. He was called the "black" because of his black hair. Not all Scandinavians are blond.

The Scandinavian kings in those days did not live in royal palaces such as the kings of France or Byzantium. They were farmers. The actual farm work, however, was mostly done by women, children, old men and slaves. Raiding, burning and stealing seemed much more fitting for them.

Halvdan's parents had a violent courtship. When his father, Gudrod, lost his first wife in death, he spotted Asa, the beautiful daughter of the king of Agder. His marriage proposal was rejected. So he raided their home, killed the royal family and kidnapped the princess. A year after Halvdan was born, Asa had her revenge. When Gudrod was drunk (drinking was a way of life for Viking kings), she had him murdered, took the child back to Agder and assumed power.

At age 18, when Scandinavians reached legal age, Halvdan claimed both Vestfold and Agder as his territory. It wasn't long before he went on raiding parties and became a "mighty king," according to Snorri Sturluson, the great saga writer.

Queen Asa has been the subject of some interesting speculation. In 1904, the Oseberg Viking ship was discovered in an ancient burial ground southwest of Oslo. It turned out to be the largest collection of objects from the Viking Age ever found in Scandinavia. Two female skeletons were in the royal ship, one about age 20 and the other about 50. It is speculated that the older woman was Queen Asa and the younger was a female slave who was buried with her alive, according to their customs.

15

The blood of two royal lines, Swedish and Danish, merged in Halvdan the Black. Asa can rightly be called the "grandmother of modern Norway," according to Magnus Magnuson, a popular writer on the sagas. She was the grandmother of King Harald Fine Hair (Haarfagre) who united Norway into a single nation.

Halvdan was considered a wise and just king. He not only made laws, and enforced them, but kept them himself. He came, however, to a tragic death. It was in the spring of the year when he was returning from a feast in Hadeland. Travelling over ice weakened by a late winter thaw, he drowned with all the people in his sledge. During the winter, cattle had been branded on the lake. Some of the dung had eaten through the ice in the warmer weather and it gave way when the king travelled over it.

They were going to bury his body in Ringerike, but the leaders of Romerike, Vestfold and Hedmark demanded equal rights. It was considered good luck for the crops to have a king buried in their territory. So they quartered him and he was buried in four provinces.

Those old pagan times were crude and cruel days. 135 years later, Olaf Tryggvason, a descendant of Halvdan, brought a new religion to Norway. The present King, Olav V, also traces his roots to Asa's son.

The Oseberg Ship.

CHAPTER 9

The Scandinavians
Of Detroit

WHEN WE GOT A FINNISH daughter-in-law from Michigan, I didn't realize how many more Scandinavians lived there. I was surprised to learn from Dordi Glaerum Skuggevik's book "Utvandringshistorie Fra Nordmore" ("Immigration History From Nordmore") how many people from Stangvik and Surnadal settled in Michigan. I suspect that if I visited in the Traverse City area, I'd find a number of distant relatives.

One of the best guarded secrets of the Middle West has to be the vigorous Scandinavian community in the Detroit area. I'm surprised they haven't renamed it "Fjord City." The Norse Civic Association was founded by the Detroit area Scandinavians in 1934. The "Nordic News," a quality publication, appears ten times a year.

Twenty-eight Scandinavian organizations hold membership in the Association. The ethnic backgrounds come from Denmark, Faroe Islands, Finland, Iceland, Norway and Sweden. Among the organizations are singing groups, folk dancers, businesswomen's club, senior citizens, stamp collectors, a Jenny Lind Club, the American-Scandinavian Foundation and the Scandinavian Symphony Society of Detroit, besides Danish, Norwegian and Swedish cultural lodges. That's impressive!

I was delightfully surprised to receive an invitation to attend their 50th anniversary meeting at the Finnish Cultural Center in Farmington Hills, a suburb of Detroit. With regrets, I could not attend.

Each month, the "Nordic News" announces special events of the various groups. I noted a well written article on how Norway got its constitution at "Syttende Mai" (17th of May) time 1984. In November 1984, there was an article on the Finnish Cultural Center. It began in a basement in 1965. Nine years later a building was dedicated. At first, it seemed foolish to make such an investment. Over 6000 Finnish-Americans were invited to discuss the project. Today 1700 families are

17

members of the Finnish Center Association. It's a handsomely designed building which does credit to Finnish architectural fame.

What impresses me most is their Scandinavian Symphony Orchestra, with both a Symphony Society and a women's auxiliary to support it. They play some pretty good music. One of their programs featured a highly talented cellist and works by Dvorak, Auber, Rossini and Hugo Alfven, a Swedish composer.

I was also interested to discover that there is a Swedish Engineer's Society of Detroit. The "Motor City" has consulate offices from each of the Scandinavian countries and they participate actively in the Association. I was also appreciative that they called attention to the "Scandinavian Heritage Calendar," which I created in 1983. Advertising is popular in the "Nordic News," especially for travel to Scandinavia.

If you have Scandinavian friends living in the Detroit area, tell them to get in touch with this interesting organization. Maybe they'll get invited to the Danish Club of Detroit for a Sunday brunch.

It's no wonder that the "Hjemkomst" Viking ship stopped in Detroit on its way to Norway in 1983. They were given a "royal" welcome. They're people worth knowing!

The Finnish Center in Detroit.

CHAPTER 10

The American
Swedish Institute

ONE OF THE PROUD PLACES in Minneapolis is the American Swedish Institute at 2600 Park Avenue. It was founded in 1929 by Swan J. Turnblad "to promote and preserve the Swedish heritage in America." It has about 7000 members. They have an excellent publication called the "ASI Posten" which appears ten times a year. The Institute is headquartered in one of the most elegant buildings in the Middle West.

Even if you don't live in Minnesota, you might want to get acquainted with this organization if you are of Swedish background or if you are interested in Scandinavian culture. However, if you live in the Twin Cities, there are many direct benefits: free admission to the museum, invitations to special events and exhibits, discounts on gift purchases, language study and travel discounts besides a subscription to the newsletter.

One of the special features to the "Posten" is the column entitled, "Sag Det Pa Svenska!" ("Say it in Swedish!") Did you know that "en forening" means "an organization" or "association?" Or that "en ordforande" means "a chairman?" Or that "en dragspelare" was "an accordion player?" By studying these columns each month, a person can gain a good working knowledge of Swedish in a couple of year's membership.

The Institute offers scholarships for young people who attend the Swedish Camp called "Sjolunden." It's a part of Concordia College's International Language Villages. Besides the two week and the four week language study programs in Minnesota, they also offer a month of travelling in Sweden.

The Institute offers classes in the Swedish language, folk art, folk fiddling and Swedish exercises. In 1985, which was the year of Bach, a special nine week class on the famous composer was held. Travel to Sweden is an important part of their ethnic heritage. The Institute promotes such tours with special rates to members.

19

As would be expected, the Swedish Lucia Festival (December 13) is a gala event in the Institute's social program. Beautiful Swedish young women dress up in their prettiest to compete for the crown. Tickets to this event are limited and every year has a sellout.

The Institute is a member of the Swedish Council of America which sponsors a "Swedish Week" and publishes a quarterly journal entitled "Sweden & America." In 1984, the "Swedish Week" was celebrated in Seattle, and His Royal Highness Prince Bertil of Sweden was awarded America's "Swede of the Year." The "Great Swedish Heritage Award" was presented to actress Ann Margret and Nobel Laureate Glenn T. Seaborg.

The Swedes are rightfully proud of Raoul Wallenberg for his heroic effort to save more than 100,000 Hungarian Jews from Nazi death camps. The Institute featured an exhibit of his work in 1985. If you are going to Minneapolis, it will be worth your time to visit this fine center of Swedish culture.

I'm proud to be a member of the Swedish-American Institute, even though my ethnic heritage is Norwegian. I have great admiration for Sweden and the Swedish heritage. So I am grateful that ASI allows us friends of Sweden and Swedish culture into their ranks. But then, I'm prejudiced. We have a charming daughter-in-law and three handsome grandsons who claim the Swedish heritage.

CHAPTER 11

'News From
Norway'

"**N**EWS FROM NORWAY" used to mean a letter from the
"Old Country" to the family in the "New World." Today
it is a newsletter issued ten times a year by the Royal Norwegian Embassy in Washington, D.C. It's edited by Sverre
Jervell who attended the 1987 Norsk Høstfest. The newsletter is available on request without cost.

This publication has interesting reports about the latest information
on Norwegian culture, politics, economics and industrial development.
It also lists titles of English publications of Norwegian interests. It even
contains recipes.

Since there are more Norwegian-Americans than there are
Norwegians in Norway, it's of special interest to the government in the
"Motherland" to maintain the friendliest of relations with the United
States. There are no countries in the world where America is held in
such high esteem as by the people as in Scandinavia, even when the
press and government disagree with some of our economic and foreign
policies.

When Norway became an oil exporting nation, its economy was in-
fused with a surge of new wealth. Rather than pump all the new money
into the nation's business, large amounts were set aside to help Third
World Countries with their development. This helped hold Norway's
inflation down.

Exporting is important to Norway. Of the 13,000 industrial firms in
the country, 1800 are active exporters. I was surprised to discover a
relative in Oslo, Thor Fiske, who has a position in this business. A country like Norway needs to export its goods to survive in the modern
world.

Norway encourages Americans to study in their universities and colleges. They also invite American high school students to attend Camp

Norway in Sandane, operated through the Minnesota Department of Education and Augsburg College in Minneapolis. At Voss, there's a summer school of fine arts for high school students. For students who want to spend a full school year in Norway, there are scholarships to attend folk high schools. Scholarships for advanced study and research are also available. "News From Norway" contains information on such study opportunities.

Shortwave radio schedules are printed in the newsletter. Radio Norway International sends out a half hour program in English called "Norway Today" every Sunday evening besides the regular Norwegian broadcasts.

Norway is a believer in its young people. They strongly supported the 1985 International Youth Year, a program of the United Nations. One interesting thing I learned from this publication is that 63% of unmarried Norwegian young people between 20 and 25 have savings accounts. Norwegian youth have strong feelings for the youth of poorer nations. They participate in "Operation One-Day-Work" which sends money to help refugees in southern Africa. In Norwegian schools there is time set aside between classes for discussion and outdoor activities. This allows students to be relaxed while in school. They believe that stress inhibits learning. All this information is in "News From Norway."

If you would like to receive this newsletter, write: Royal Norwegian Embassy, 2720 - 34th Street, N.W., Washington, D.C. 20008.

Royal Norwegian
Coat of Arms.

CHAPTER 12

Church Life
In Norway

THERE ARE THREE SIGNIFICANT periods in Norway's
church life: the High Middle Ages (1000-1300), the Reformation era beginning in 1536 and the Modern period from
about 1800.

Norway became a part of "Christendom" through the conquest of
King Olaf Haraldson ("St. Olaf") starting in 1014. In this period, the
Christian religion became the law of the land and the church a vast land
owner. Dissent was dangerous. Pilgrimages and the crusades were held
to be the surest way of gaining salvation.

The Reformation came to Norway first at Bergen through the Hanse
merchants from Germany. By 1536, Lutheranism replaced the authority
of Rome. The King in Copenhagen appointed the bishops and took over
the church lands. He also had St. Olaf's casket removed from Trondheim
to Denmark where it is thought that the jewels were removed and the
silver melted down for the king's treasury. His remains were buried
somewhere either in the cathedral or on the grounds. That ended the
cult of Olaf and the pilgrimages to his grave.

The "Great Awakening" of the Norwegian church began with a
farmer from southeast of Oslo, Hans Nielsen Hauge. Born in 1771,
Hauge grew up in a pious home and parish. It was, however, a brooding
and melancholy faith with lots of emotion and sentimentalism. Hauge's
problem with that piety was its lack of ethical seriousness.

Much like John Wesley's conversion, Hauge claimed a spiritual
breakthrough when he was 25 years old, telling him "you shall confess
my Name before men." Hauge was faithful to his vision. He preached
his message of faith and moral earnestness in every community which
he could reach. Though opposed by the authorities, he made a mark
on Norway unequalled by any other person, bringing an awakening to
the land which deeply influenced immigrants going to the New World.

Until the Oslo University opened in 1813, Norway's clergy were trained in Copenhagen. Among the outstanding church leaders in the 19th century were Prof. Gisle Johnson of Icelandic background; Prof. Carl Paul Caspari, a German Jew who converted to Lutheranism; and Bishop J. C. Heuch, who wrote an excellent book on pastoral care. Norway has had its share of the "liberal" and "conservative" struggle. As a result, two theological faculties in Oslo prepare candidates for the ministry, the independent ("Menighetsfakultetet," "congregational faculty") and the state university.

Foreign mission work has been a passion for the church in Norway. South Africa, Madagascar and China were early areas of activity. The mission societies raise significant sums of money for this work.

Fortunately, the leaders of the church came to an agreement in the 1930s, just in time to be united against the Nazi occupation which tried to control the clergy. The best known leader was Bishop Eivind Berggrav, whose family traced its roots to Germany. A "reformed liberal," he took a strong stand on the church's confession of faith and became a symbol of resistance for the whole nation. I saw him several times during the 1950s.

Despite many predictions that the church of Norway has suffered a demise, my own observation is that the church is deeply rooted in the consciousness of the people and has its greatest influence whenever the nation feels itself in danger.

CHAPTER 13

The Oslo
Cathedral

I T WAS NOT UNTIL ADULT YEARS that I learned why my home
congregation in Colfax, North Dakota, is named "Our Saviour's."
Called "Vor Frelsers Menighed" in Norwegian, it took its name
from the Cathedral Church in Oslo. The original Our Saviour's
Church, consecrated on November 7, 1697, which replaced Holy Trinity
Church, built in 1630 and which burned in 1686. Before Holy Trinity's
time, there was St. Hallvard's, built about 1100 and burned in 1624. In
those days, fires were a constant threat to cities.

The present church building has been twice renovated. First re-done
in 1849-50, the latest renewal was completed in 1950 to celebrate Oslo's
900th anniversary. Two massive bronze doors designed by Dagfin
Werenskiold portraying the Beatitudes greet the visitor. The hand carved
altar, designed in Renaissance and Baroque patterns, shows the Last
Supper and Crucifixion, with St. John and the Holy Mother standing
on each side of the cross. At the top is a carving of the Risen Christ
flanked by two angels. The pulpit was carved by a Dutch craftsman and
was placed in the church in 1699. At the top of the canopy above the
pulpit is the King's monogram - C 5 - standing for Christian V. By it
are two lions. These carvings have become an inspiration to woodcarvers all over Norway. Woodcarving is a national hobby in this land
of forests.

The first organ was built in 1711 by a famous Danish organ-builder,
Lambert Daniel Karsten. It was renovated in 1930. In 1976, a new organ
was installed which has 87 stops and five manuals plus pedal.

Sixteen stained glass windows are the work of Emanuel Vigeland,
a famous name among Norwegian artists. Showing scenes from both
Old and New Testaments, they were given as a memorial to those killed
in World War II. There are also pictures of St. Augustine, St. Bernhard,
Luther and Calvin.

The most spectacular art work is on the ceilings. These were completed in 1950. They tell the story of the Bible. The paintings are based on the Apostles' Creed and can be seen from below at any angle.

A small chapel was completed in 1950. One of the stained glass windows was donated in memory of Crown Princess Martha (1901-54), wife of King Olav V.

Our Saviour's Cathedral is probably the most ornately decorated church in Norway. Every detail has been planned to help the worshipper meet Jesus Christ as "Lord of the universe."

In front of the church is a statue of the Danish King, Christian IV, who rebuilt Oslo after the great fire of 1624. Nearby is an open market. But let me advise you, if you go looking for the cathedral, follow your street directions carefully. None of the streets are straight. If you get lost, just walk downhill. It will take you straight to the harbor and then you can start all over again. The clock on the tower was installed in 1718, the oldest in the country and it still works.

If you go to Oslo, visit Our Saviour's Church for a worship service and stay for a guided tour. It's part of the Scandinavian heritage. It's well worth an extra hour of your time.

Bronze doors at the entrance of Oslo Cathedral.

CHAPTER 14

The Town Hall
In Oslo

OSLO HAS MANY PLACES OF BEAUTY. When I walk along Karl Johansgate, the street which leads from the palace to the parliament building, a good and strange feeling comes over me. It's where the Syttende Mai (17th of May) parade takes place each year. The pride of the city, however, is the "Radhus," (Town Hall), about three blocks south, across the highway from the harbor.

The Town Hall was opened on May 15, 1950, when Oslo celebrated its 900th anniversary. Thousands of tourists from all over the world come each year to gaze at its lofty ceilings and admire its famous art work.

The twin towered structure is built of red brick and stands where a permanent circus stood in the old days. Once there were a lot of tumbledown houses lining the harbor, but today it is a spectacle of beauty. It is to the credit of a former mayor, Hieronimus Heyerdahl, that the improvement project got underway. The work was approved in 1917 and a contest was held throughout Norway for ideas on the planning.

Architects were commissioned in 1920, but it took until September 4, 1931, before the foundation was laid. Many obstacles stood in the way. Norway had been an independent country only since 1905 and the world economy was in trouble. World War II brought everything to a halt. The building now houses the municipal offices and many of the nation's art treasures. The sculptures and paintings are worth taking time to see. They are massive and overwhelming.

King Harald Hardrade, who once led the Varangian Guard in Constantinople, protects one wall of the Radhus. The courtyard is flanked with scenes of the Old Norse Eddas (mythology).

The "Main Hall" is the showpiece of Oslo. The south wall shows Henrik Sorensen's mural of the nation at work and play. It's a panorama of Norwegian life. On the east wall is the "Occupation Frieze," showing the struggle for freedom from 1940-1945. Other scenes depict the "Labor Movement" and "The Commerce and Industry of the City."

I especially like the Corner Room with Edvard Munch's painting of "Life." Munch was an internationally recognized artist whose work shows deep emotion, often on the darker side. In the Festival Gallery, there are scenes from the different regions of Norway. It's hard to imagine how much variation there is in Norway's scenery and climate. In one respect, however, there is total agreement. This is found in a painting of His Majesty King Haakon VII in the Banquet Hall. Haakon VII was king from 1905 to 1958 and is the symbol of Norway's freedom.

The "Town Council Chamber" is designed in a semi-round with lightly stained modernistic furniture, surrounded by orange-red wood panelled walls. Behind the chairman's desk is a huge tapestry with more scenes of Norwegian life. Most touching of all is the decorated tree that stands in the City Hall during the Christmas season. The City Hall is a must for every visitor in Oslo to see. It's more than an office building. It embodies the spirit of freedom, held dear by Norwegians everywhere. Don't miss it if you visit Oslo.

Oslo City Hall.

CHAPTER 15

A. M. Andersen —
Pathfinder For Dana College

W HEN WE TOOK OUR SON, PAUL, to enroll in Dana College at Blair, Nebraska, in 1971, I was impressed by the "Old Main" building on the campus. It isn't large by the standards of college buildings today, but it somehow said that this college had a place where its heart was located.

It was not until later that I learned the story of Pastor A. M. Andersen, the man who was the "pathfinder" for this Danish school on the plains of Nebraska. Andersen was born March 8, 1847, in Denmark. One of seven children, he learned the weaver's trade. After serving his military obligation, he told his family that he wanted to be a pastor. Despite the fact that they were a pious family, his father became so angry that he disinherited him. His pastor advised him to go to America and go to school with other Danes there.

In the spring of 1872, Andersen went to Wisconsin where he worked on a farm. That fall, he enrolled at Augsburg Seminary in Minneapolis. During summers, he taught "parochial" (religious) school and preached to Danish settlers. In 1874, Andersen was ordained and went to Dannebrog in eastern Nebraska to work among the Danes.

Those were not easy days on the frontier. Roads were only trails across the prairies with few, if any, bridges. One of his missions was 100 miles away, another 120 miles. After a year and a half, he moved to Racine, Wisconsin, still regarded as the most Danish city in the United States. In another three and a half years he was back in Nebraska.

Andersen's most important work was in Blair, about 30 miles north of Omaha. Blair became a center of Danish culture. (Johnny Carson often refers to Blair as his hometown on the "Tonight Show".) In 1884, Andersen founded Trinity Seminary, teaching most of the classes on the second floor of his home during the first year. If Danish pastors were going to give pastoral care to Danish immigrants, it was important to

29

have their own seminary in those days. Otherwise, these immigrants would join mostly non-Danish congregations. Many of them did anyway. The "Old Main" was built in 1886 at a cost of $7000, of which $3000 was given by the people of Blair. In 1956, Trinity Seminary moved to Dubuque, Iowa, and was merged with Wartburg Seminary. Dana College, however, remains in Blair.

In 1899, a Danish folk high school and college from Elk Horn, Iowa, merged with Trinity Seminary and became known as "Dana College." Dana has never been a large school (about 500 plus students), but it has had loyal support from the Danish communities in the United States. Dana is highly respected wherever it's known. One of its prominent alumni is Senator Paul Simon of Illinois, who was a presidential hopeful in early 1988.

Andersen was short on formal education, but he proved to be a creative and energetic leader. He became editor of "Danskeren," a Danish church publication. Andersen helped organize the Blair school board and served on it for many years. A deeply religious and temperate man, he would refuse a second helping of food, saying, "I have had adequate food for this meal."

Denmark's King Christian X recognized Andersen with the "Golden Cross of the Royal Order of the Knights of Dannebrog." At age 91, Dana College presented him with an honorary doctorate. Friends of the Danish-American heritage continue to honor A. M. Andersen, the "pathfinder" for Dana College.

CHAPTER 16

Knute Nelson —
Champion Of Children's Rights

KNUTE NELSON (1843-1923) WAS THE first Norwegian immigrant to become a state senator, congressman, governor and U.S. Senator in the New World. In Washington,- Nelson used his influence to enact some of the most significant legislation ever to become law in our land.

Who was Knute Nelson and what kind of a beginning did he have? Born in the district of Voss at Evanger, Norway, his mother brought him to America in 1849 when he was only six years old. For a short time they lived in the new city of Chicago, but times were tough and they moved to La Grange, Wisconsin. There his mother married Nels Nelson, also an immigrant, and Knute was given his new father's name. In 1853 they moved to Deerfield, about 20 miles east of Madison.

When Knute was 15, he entered nearby Albion Academy where he worked for his tuition and room. He brought food and fuel from home. Then he taught school. When the war between the states came, he enlisted in the Union Army and fought at Vicksburg and New Orleans. Later wounded, he was a prisoner for a month.

After the war, Knute studied law with a lawyer in Madison and was admitted to the bar in 1867, the same year he was married. Politics drew him into public life, beginning with the state legislature in Wisconsin. In 1871, he moved to Alexandria, Minnesota, frontier country in those days. Combining homesteading and law, he was soon back in politics, becoming county attorney and a state senator. Washington beckoned Nelson to Congress in 1882 for three terms. Then he quit. But in 1892, the Republicans elected him governor to try to keep the Scandinavians from joining the Populist Party. Elected twice, he resigned when named by the legislature to be a United States Senator. He was re-elected until he died.

When Theodore Roosevelt was president, the Nelson amendment to a bill establishing the Department of Commerce and Labor began

31

sweeping reforms in child labor laws. Roosevelt wanted authority to publicize information about the wrongdoings of large corporations. John D. Rockefeller sent telegrams to six key Senators opposing the bill. The bill passed the House by 252 to 10 on Feb. 10, 1903.

More than 1,500,000 children worked for as little as 25 cents a day in 1900. In one case, a mother reported: "The boss was good; he let me off early the night baby was born." In three days she was back at work with the baby in a little box on a pillow beside the loom. Children of six became wage earners and snuff sniffers. There is evidence to claim that much of America's wealth in the 19th century was bought at the price of children's toil. When confronted, the owners threatened to close the mines and mills.

Nelson, a short man of broad stature and whose chin whiskers turned gray early, became known as the "grand old man of Minnesota. He lived a simple lifestyle. Not only Minnesota, but the nation is in debt to this immigrant boy. In his lifetime, he was the best known Norwegian in America. Today his statue stands in front of the State Capitol in St. Paul.

L. GAYLOR

Norwegian Immigrant Children.

CHAPTER 17

Orion Samuelson —
'Voice Of American Agriculture'

"**A**FTER LIVING ON A FARM for my first 21 years, I got tired of getting up at 5:30 to milk cows. So I went off to school to become a radio announcer. Now I get up at 3:30." That's what Orion Samuelson, the "Voice of American Agriculture," told me.

You can listen to Samuelson as early as 4:50 a.m. (Central time) on the radio. Together with his associate, Max Armstrong, they broadcast 14 daily agri-business reports Monday through Saturday until 9:00 p.m. When I lived in Chicago, I heard him several times a day over WGN ("World's Greatest Newspaper" - the station is owned by the Chicago Tribune). This 50,000 watt Clear Channel station carries Samuelson's voice to millions of listeners.

Besides radio, WGN-TV brings Samuelson's "National Farm Report" to 300 radio stations. Besides radio broadcasting, Samuelson's "U.S. Farm Report" is telecast on 140 stations across the country, plus an additional 7000 cable systems in North America. His broadcasts reach out to 23-million homes.

Starting out in a one-room country grade school near Sparta, Wisconsin, Orion developed "Legg-Calve-Perthes" disease at age 14. This is an ailment in which the bone around the hip joint decays. During the first summer, he was in a body cast, flat on his back. He listened to Cub baseball games on WLS and decided to be a radio announcer. After two years of convalescing in a wheel chair and with crutches, he got his public speaking training through FFA.

In high school, Samuelson worked the public address system for basketball games. Then he entered the University of Wisconsin for radio training. They wanted to make a writer out of him. Orion said, "No, thanks," and went to Brown Institute in Minneapolis. After six months, he took a job at the Sparta station. He still had to get up at 5:30 and milk cows before going to work. Then he moved up to Appleton and

33

Green Bay. Big time - WGN in Chicago - came in 1960 when the station's regular farm broadcaster joined John F. Kennedy's Presidential campaign.

In 1975, Samuelson was elected Vice President of Continental Broadcasting Company, WGN's parent. He has been honored by almost every major farm organization in the nation. He's especially proud of his recognitions by the National 4-H and FFA. He is the only broadcaster to receive two "Oscars" in agriculture, one in radio and one in TV.

Travelling more than 65,000 miles per year, Samuelson's advice is often sought by U.S. Secretaries of Agriculture. In August 1983, he was with John Block as media observer when the U.S./U.S.S.R. Grain Agreement was signed in Moscow. He has also been to the Far East and Great Britain. He is a master of ceremonies for more than 100 meetings a year, including President Reagen's 1984 "Hometown Birthday Party" in Dixon, IL.

Samuelson has received many recognitions and awards during his career. He has been recognized by the American Soybean Association, the National Association of Soil & Water Conservation Districts, American Communicators in Education, the Dairy Nutrition Council, and was named "Chicagoan of the Year in Agriculture" by the Chicago Jaycees, besides being named National Farm broadcaster of the Year.

His foreign travels on behalf of agriculture have taken him to Scotland, England, Hungary, France, Denmark, Norway, Sweden, Austria, Canada, Mexico, Japan, Korea, Taiwan, Hong Kong, Philippines, Thailand, People's Republic of China and the U.S.S.R.

He is Vice Chairman of the Board of Directors of the Illinois Agricultural Leadership Foundation, a member of the Illinois State Fair Advisory Board and has been President of the National Association of Farm Broadcasters Foundations since 1975. He has also served on the Chicago Board of Trade and the FFA Foundation Sponsor Committee. It's difficult to measure his influence on agriculture except to say it has been outstanding.

Samuelson's interests are not limited to agriculture. He has been Chairman of the Board of Deacons for Trinity Lutheran Church in Evanston, IL, and served seven years on the Board of Governors for the

Lutheran General Medical Center in Park Ridge, IL, when I was teaching there.

Minot's Norsk Høstfest Association honored this son of Norwegian immigrants by inducting him into the "Scandinavian-American Hall of Fame" in 1985. He represents the best in the Scandinavian heritage.

Orion Samuelson.

CHAPTER 18

The Scandinavians
Are Coming!

THEY'RE COMING! The Scandinavians are coming to America in record numbers for these times. Not to plunder or immigrate, but to sing, to play their mountain folk songs, for soccer tournaments and to learn what became of the people that left the "Fatherlands." They save their money all year long with the dream of visiting the "New World."

The dollar value is turning in their favor too. When I visited the "old country" in 1977, the dollar bought five Norwegian crowns (krone) or six Danish. Swedish money was about four to one. In 1985, the dollar was worth over ten Danish crowns and about eight and a half Norwegian or Swedish crowns. It's a good time for Scandinavians to come to America.

A few years ago, a boy's soccer team from Lorenskog (suburb of Oslo), came to North Dakota to play the best teams in the state. They didn't lose a game. They did, however, make a lot of friends and left behind a few sad hearts. The American girls thought blonde hair and blue eyes handsome.

One of the most famous singing groups in Norway is the Silver Boy's Choir (Solvguttenes) from Oslo. In 1982, they sang for the Norsk Høstfest in Minot, ND and in 1983 they sang for a Tchaikovsky Festival in Moscow. To my surprise, I discovered a distant relative in the choir who had our family name. We later visited his home in Oslo.

Another group to visit the Norsk Høstfest was the Fjellklang Spelemannslag from Jolster and Breim in the "Vestlands" (Westlands). They have brought to life many of the old songs that had almost been forgotten. In 1984, we stopped at a hotel cafeteria for lunch in Skei, between Balestrand and Horindal. When the owner, Jon Skrede, heard we were from Minot, he became quite excited. He had been one of the Spelemannslag musicians to visit our city.

Typical of these groups is the "Ganddal Pikekor" (Girls Choir, pronounced "peek-a-core") from Sandnes, county of Rogaland, in southwest Norway. Started in 1960, the choir consists of 20 girls, ages 19-25. They have performed in many countries of Europe, the Far East and in New Zealand, winning many awards. Their selections include classical works, folks songs, hymns and spirituals. They prefer to sing in churches and stay in homes. Their 1985 tour divided into two groups and covered a great of the United States, inlcluding Chicago and the Middle West, including North Dakota, Colorado, Texas and Florida. Accompanying one of the Gandal groups on the piano was a brilliant young Norwegian pianist named Geir Botnen from Norheimsund. (See Chapter 100.)

Not only do these beautiful young ladies have well trained voices, but they sing in their native costumes called "bunads." These dresses are made of pure wool, with hand made embroidery and silver brooches. Each valley has its own distinctive pattern. These clothes, which symbolize former days, get a little warm in our American summers.

Whenever one of these Scandinavian singing groups comes to your community, they deserve a good audience. The Ganddal singers have been to Minot twice in recent years. Singing in both English and Scandinavian, they won our hearts. I hope the Scandinavians will keep coming.

Norwegian soccer player in America.

CHAPTER 19

An Evening With
Victor Borge

VICTOR BORGE CAME TO MINOT, ND, to put on his program of music and comedy for the Norsk Høstfest in October
1984. My wife and I were his hosts. When asked by the
press if he had been looking forward to the event, he answered: "Yes, I've been looking forward to it all my life." From the moment he arrived at the airport, he kept people guessing what he would
say next.

Despite his international fame as an entertainer, Borge is a very plain
appearing person. He travelled with his son who was his business agent.
There was no entourage with dozens of suitcases. He speaks with the
inimitable Danish accent that I have come to appreciate in my wife's
family. Try as I will, I can't make my Norwegian sound Danish. While
dining together, I noted that he followed a simple diet.

Borge has complete communication with his audience. He claims he
doesn't plan his programs in advance. He knows what he can do, but
waits until he walks out on to the stage to decide what it will be. He
singled out people in the audience and involved them in the program.
A freelance photographer moved towards the stage when Borge stopped his routine, saying: "You want my picture? Here." Then he pulled
a press release photo out of his coat pocket and gave it to him. It was
not possible to tell if he welcomed the interruption or if it irritated him.
After the concert, he told us that it was an irritation.

The famed Dane is not all comedy. Underneath is a person who is
serious. During breakfast the next morning, we talked about nuclear
sanity and world peace. He is deeply concerned about the future of the
world and the good of other people.

Born Borge Rosenbaum on January 3, 1909 to a musical family in
Copenhagen, he gave his first recital when eight. At age 14, he was one
of the first European pianists to perform Rachmaninoff's Second Piano
Concerto. When the conductor began beating the wrong time, Borge

38

walked to the podium and pointed out the maestro's error. Then throwing a smile and a wink to the audience, he returned to the piano. That launched his career in comedy.

Fortunately for Borge, he was in Sweden on May 9, 1940, when Hitler invaded Denmark. The Nazis didn't find his jokes about Der Fuehrer funny. Both his humor and his Jewish heritage became a target of Nazi threats. He caught the last ship out of Finland in order to come to America, where he began a new career with Bing Crosby on the Kraft Music Hall.

Many governments have "knighted" the Danish virtuoso. He quipped, "now finally, I have enough knights for two weekends." His books are sold at concerts. I bought "My Favorite Intermissions." It's a humorous biographical sketch of the great musicians. It reminds me of a book I read over 30 years ago entitled "The Rise and Fall of Practically Everybody." His favorite piano is the Bosendorfer. It has 97 keys instead of the usual 88 and costs over $50,000.

People wonder if Borge ever plays a whole piece through. I asked if he would be doing this at the Høstfest performance. He answered, "We'll see," and he did. Even at age 75, he was still a pro and he made it an evening to remember. I hope he returns for another concert.

Victor Borge.

CHAPTER 20

My Unforgettable
Swedish Friend

I T WAS FEBRUARY 1964 IN ST. LOUIS. The telephone rang, "This is the International Institute calling. There is a young man here from Sweden who is very lonesome. Would you talk with him?" This began an unusual and interesting friendship that has continued ever since.

Elon Eliasson (Ay-lon Ay-lee-a-son) telephones me at unpredictable times. He used to begin: "Dis is da King!" I'd know his voice anywhere and any time. It's unforgettable.

A native of Gothenborg on Sweden's west coast (where Saab automobiles are manufactured), Elon served in the Swedish navy with Ingemar Johansson, former world heavyweight boxing champion (1959-60). They were good friends and had travelled together in China when no Americans were allowed into the country.

I took Elon to our home in Webster Groves (a suburb to the southwest of St. Louis) where he became acquainted with my family. He was a great entertainer. The children had never seen anyone walk on their hands before. Elon had heard a lot about Chicago gangsters, especially Al Capone. It's no wonder he carried a blackjack in his pocket for protection. One can't be too careful in a strange land.

What brought this Swede to the "Gateway City" of America? Elon was trained as a chef in Paris under a famous teacher. His first job in the U.S. was at the Waldorf Astoria in New York. His sense of adventure brought him to Trader Vics in St. Louis, a famous Polynesian eating place. He wanted to learn English, but discovered he was working with 27 Chinese cooks. A friend of mine, Jack Eriksen, now retired in Billings, Montana, was an engineer at the Missouri Athletic Club. He helped Elon get work at the club so he could become Americanized.

One day, Elon asked us to sponsor his fiancee, Norah Gustafson, to the America. A few weeks later, I officiated at their wedding. The service was done in both Norwegian and English (I didn't have a Swedish liturgy). Afterwards he said, "I was married twice." The reception was at the Bevo Mill in south St. Louis, where Mayor Cervantes stopped each morning to visit with friends. They came to church services every Sunday and stayed for dinner at our house. He liked our food, but used to complain that American coffee was too weak. One time he ran it through the filter a second time. They also put on a Swedish dinner for our congregation. It was a work of art.

Today Elon and Norah operate a delicatessen in White Plains, NY, just above Manhattan. For a few years he was head chef at a private club where Henry Kissinger was a member. He used to bake Nelson Rockefeller's birthday cake.

Norah is also a professional food preparer, a specialist in "kaltbord" (cold table). I've been a guest in their home and was treated royally with Scandinavian hospitality. If you are going to New York City and want to have some authentic Scandinavian food, be sure to visit their shop called "Gourmet Delight" in White Plains. Just tell them that I told you to stop in. You'll like these fine people. Some day our phone will ring again and it will be my unforgettable Swedish friend, wondering if I'm still alive.

CHAPTER 21

T. G. Mandt — "Wagonmaker"

MANY PEOPLE KNOW THAT Stoughton, Wisconsin, has been called "The most Norwegian city in America," but few may be aware of the man who brought it so much fame. His name was T. (Targe) G. Mandt. Born in 1845 in Telemarken County, Norway, he came to Dane County, Wisconsin, when just two years old.

During the Civil War, Mandt wanted to join the army, but was too young. So he went to St. Joseph, Missouri, and got a job making wagons for the Union forces. He became so good at it that after the war he moved to Stoughton and began making wagons to sell. Only 19 and with just $40 in his pocket, he was convinced that he could build a better wagon than anyone else. According to thousands of farmers in Wisconsin, Minnesota, Iowa and the Dakotas, he did.

During the years 1873-75, hard times came to the farmers. Grasshoppers descended like a biblical plague. It looked like the end for Mandt as the creditors came to collect. He didn't have bankruptcy laws to protect him, but Mandt wouldn't have used them anyway. Because of his good reputation, the creditors agreed to take 35 cents on a dollar. Even though he had his receipts marked "paid in full," Mandt paid his creditors every cent he had owed when the business bounced back. It was that kind of honesty that went into making his wagon a quality product.

It wasn't long before the wagon works became Stoughton's busiest business. This is also the reason why so many Norwegians flocked to this city which still has one of the best "Syttende Mai" (17th of May) celebrations in the nation. By 1883, 225 men worked for Mandt. Then tragedy struck. On Saturday. January 13, 1883, fire destroyed almost the whole plant. It looked bad for everyone in the city.

But Mandt was not a quitter. He had been travelling when the plant burned. Upon his return, he gave orders to rebuild immediately. Within a week, orders were being filled again. His massive frame and seemingly endless human energy set a good example to all his workers. He was also generous and gave frequent gifts to charity. On Christmas Day 1901, he collected $500 for the orphan's home in just a few hours.

As a manufacturer of wagons, sleighs and carriages, Mandt's motto was "The Best is the Cheapest." People used to say they could tell a Mandt wagon when they met it because it didn't rattle. In the last year of his life, he built 15,000 wagons and sleighs. He died Feb. 28, 1902. The people of Stoughton remember their famous citizen with pride. If you drive past there sometime while travelling between Madison and Chicago, take an hour or so to visit this fine community.

I remember the wagons. In the Fall, we'd put our Model T up on blocks. Wagons and the sleighs were our transportation to town as well as what got me to school on many cold mornings. I thought those were fun times. Sometimes I feel we lost something pretty good when we put away that equipment which was built with such honesty and charm. They were a little slow moving, but we had a ringside seat to prairie life as we rolled along those trails.

CHAPTER 22

'Hap' Lerwick —
From Lumberjack To Surgeon

WE FIRST MET IN 1963 when he performed surgery for my brother. Dr. Everett R. Lerwick soon became special to our family both because of his outstanding medical skills and because he was a Norwegian in St. Louis. There weren't many of us in that metropolitan area.

Hap's father moved from Kristiansund on Norway's west coast to Oregon. As a young man, the future surgeon worked in lumbercamps during the summer to earn money to prepare for his profession. It was there that he earned his nickname of "Hap" by his cheerful disposition.

He studied at the University of Oregon, University of Missouri Medical School and Washington University in St. Louis. Then followed a stint with the military in Korea (1950-52). After a plastic surgery residency in Philadelphia, he returned to St. Louis where he has been Chairman of the Department of Surgery at Missouri Baptist Hospital since 1960.

His travels for lecturing and performing vascular surgeries have taken him to Brazil, Mexico, Germany, France, Italy, Sweden and Norway. The last time I visited with him, he was still excited over his 1983 trip to Stavanger to teach Norwegian surgeons.

It's not uncommon for a St. Louis newspaper to carry a story about one of Lerwick's surgeries. He designed a "Roto-Rooter that unclogs arteries. A 64-year-old man had unbearable pains in his foot. Using the instrument called the "Hall Arterial Oscillator," he cleared the arterial plaque that was keeping blood from circulating in the limb. The man walked again without pain.

A 70-year-old man was helping his son cut firewood when he was accidentally pulled into a 30 inch blade, which cut through over half of his body. He was able to say: "I want to go to Missouri Baptist and I want Dr. Lerwick." Hap was in a shopping mall buying a shirt when

44

the hospital reached him. The surgery took seven hours and 14 pints of blood. An assisting surgeon said, "This man should not have lived to even get to the hospital. I've never heard of anyone surviving such a wound." He is doing well today.

Lerwick had great appreciation for his father, also a physician. He invited me to his home so I could visit with his father in Norwegian. I took along our son, Michael, to play the violin. Our daughter, Lisa, also came along just to smile. He was a delightful gentleman and lived well into his 90s.

A new Lerwick Clinic opened November 15, 1985, in downtown St. Louis next to the famed Arch. It's modelled after the Mayo Clinic in Rochester, MN, where patients can get all their diagnostic tests under one roof. It's open 24 hours a day. Six million dollars was spent to renovate a 90 year old bank building. One of the programs gives patients a risk assessment on how to live longer. Blood chemistry, body fat, diet, weight, blood pressure, smoking habits, stress test results and age will be measured against risk factors such as cancer and heart disease.

Lerwick makes surgery look easy. But he also raises cattle in hopes of developing a breed with a leaner meat. You just wonder what he will think of next.

Our cousins in Norway are always interested in what became of those who emigrated to America. When I shared this story with Magne Holten, a local journalist from Surnadal, a valley to the southwest of Trondheim, he wrote an article in the Driva newspaper speculating that the origin of the Lerwick family was from Lervik in Valsoyfjord not far from Kristiansund. Wherever he hails from, may there be many more of his kind in both Norway and America.

CHAPTER 23

'Snowshoe' Thompson
Carries The Mail

BEFORE THE "PONY EXPRESS" carried mail over the Sierra Nevadas, a young Norwegian from Telemark sailed on skis across 90 miles of stormy heights from Placerville, California, to Carson Valley, Nevada. For twenty years, John A. Thompson, known as "Snowshoe" Thompson, carried the mail over the mountains to isolated camps, rescued lost people and helped those in need. He was a legend in his own time.

Born April 30, 1827, he emigrated to America with his mother when he was ten. After living in Illinois, Missouri and Iowa, he joined the gold-seekers in California when he was 21. He was lonesome for the mountains. Anyone who has been in Telemark knows how much mountains are a part of the people's lives.

Having moved to California, Thompson bought a ranch in the Sacramento Valley. He didn't care for a miner's life. His is believed to be the first farm owned by a Norwegian in California.

He read about the difficulty of getting mail across the Sierras and volunteered for the job. Made from oak trees on his farm, his skis were over ten feet long and weighed 25 pounds. People laughed at them and said they wouldn't work. Today they are in a Sacramento museum.

Thompson skied up to 45 miles a day over snowdrifts 50 feet deep with a load of 60 to 100 pounds on his back. Travelling light, he carried only some crackers and dried meats to eat. He did not use liquor, but scooped up snow to drink if no mountain stream was nearby. Wearing just a mackinaw, he had no blanket to keep warm. More than once Thompson jigged until morning to stay alive. Nor did he carry a weapon for protection against wolves or grizzlies. Once eight wolves blocked his path. When he didn't flinch, they let him pass. The stars and his wits were his compass.

Snow in the Sierras was deep, sometimes higher than the trees. Many mornings Snowshoe had to dig himself out of a snow bank to continue his journey. When travelling to Washington, D.C., in 1874, the train became stuck in snow so that four locomotives could not pull it through. He took to his skis and in two days had travelled the 56 miles to Cheyenne, Wyoming, beating the train.

What was his pay for 20 years of work? Many promises, but the government's response was, "We're sorry, but . . ." Later investigation into the Postmaster General's records indicated that they had not even noted his name, only his route and the dates.

For all his fame, he was a modest man, never boasting or sitting on his haunches. He is regarded today as the the most remarkable man to have ever buckled ski straps in America. One postmaster claimed he saw Thompson jump 180 feet without a break. When just 49, he died of a liver ailment on his California ranch. He is buried in Diamond Valley, 30 miles south of Carson City, beside his only son who died at age 11.

Thompson is still remembered by family in America. Janet Erdman of Willow City, North Dakota, wrote me that her grandfather, John Sanderson, was Showshoe's nephew. Like so many children of immigrants, they're proud of their Scandinavian heritage and glad to be Americans.

CHAPTER 24

Rasmus B. Anderson
And King Frederick's Pipe

RASMUS B. ANDERSON (1846-1936) was proud of his pipe. It had once belonged to Denmark's King Frederick VII. But Anderson's story is a proud chapter in Scandinavian American heritage, even without the pipe.

He was born in Koshkonong, one of the two earliest Norwegian settlements in Wisconsin. His father had owned a small trading vessel in southwest Norway. He was a born rebel. Besides being a "Quaker," he helped promote "America Fever" in Norway. Rasmus' mother was from a prominent military family, as her name "Von Krogh" might indicate. Her grand-uncle was the commander of the Norwegian armies. When she married a peasant, there was nothing to do but go to America.

Jens was only four years old when his father died of cholera, which descended upon communities like a plague in those days. His mother was a cousin of Mrs. A. C. Preus, the wife of a pioneer Koshkonong pastor. Through her influence, young Rasmus entered the first class of Luther College (1861) when it was called "Half Way Creek Academy" in Wisconsin. The school had a Spartan beginning. The parsonage served as the campus. A boy's school, the students all slept, dressed, wrote, recited and visited in one upstairs room.

Humble beginnings need not be a limiting factor for a person's growth and development. There are many of us who got our early education in one-room country schools. It was there that Rasmus began the study of languages, math, history, literature and other courses that were to prepare him to become the first Scandinavian in America to be appointed to a diplomatic office. He became the U.S. ambassador to Denmark in 1885. He was also a distinguished professor at the University of Wisconsin.

While in Copenhagen, Anderson became friends with a Jewish writer named Adler, who had bought a pipe at an auction that once belonged to King Frederick VII. When he was about to return to America, Adler

48

gave it to him as a present.

How did the pipe come to be sold? Usually these things are kept as mementos and put in museums. King Frederick VII had expected to be Norway's first king after the constitution was signed May 17, 1814. But the British had forced the Danish king to sign Norway over to Sweden after the Napoleonic wars. So Christian Frederick, as he was called, had to return to Denmark and wait his turn to become king there. He did one remarkable thing. He gave Denmark a constitution in 1848, like the one he helped Norway to obtain. It surprised people because the Danish kings were "absolutists," rulers without a constitution.

The royal family wasn't a bit pleased when he married a dressmaker. She had all the natural qualifications to be queen, except blood line. It was a happy marriage. When they died, their possessions, soiled by the hands of a commoner, were sold at a public auction.

Anderson understood the royal snub, since his mother had also fallen from favor by marrying below her class. So when a good friend came to visit him, he'd hand him the royal pipe and say, "Take a puff and be a king."

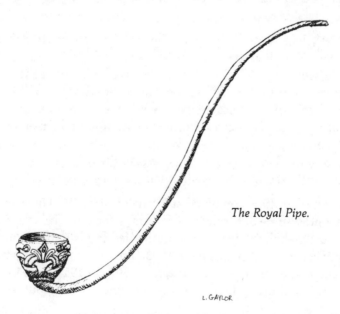

The Royal Pipe.

L. GAYLOR

CHAPTER 25

Jens Hanson And
The Vatican Library

JENS HANSON WAS ONLY NINE in the summer of 1873, when a relative from America was visiting in Valders. The visitor, Rev. Ove Hjort of Paint Creek, Iowa, asked Jens' father, a government official, to send one of his seven children back with him to America. Jens was selected to make the trip and was promised that he would be able to attend Luther College in Decorah. Thirty-four years were to pass before he would return to Norway. He never saw his parents again.

Travelling through Chicago, Jens kept a wary eye for bandits, for even at that time they had an international reputation. Arriving in Decorah, he was given private instruction. The following year, he was admitted to Luther College at age ten. That may be a record for the school. Though young, Hanson remembered college with a great deal of fondness, especially sports.

In 1882, Jens went to study at Concordia Seminary in St. Louis. It was common in those days for the Norwegian Synod students to study at the Missouri Synod school. But after two years, he realized that he ought not be a pastor. So he took a job teaching in a Norwegian parochial school on Chicago's northwest side. One time, he arranged a wrestling match between a Chicago champion and a member of the church's Young People's Society. Being the only one present who knew the rules of modern wrestling, he was also the referee. For this he was severely criticized in a Norwegian language newspaper.

Hanson's education continued at Cornell University. There he studied history under some of the best professors of the time. He was also Cornell's star baseball pitcher. These studies led to his joining the staff of the University of Wisconsin in 1893. From there he became chief cataloger at the Library of Congress in 1897. In 1910, Jens joined the University of Chicago Library staff where he rounded out his career.

One of his most interesting assignments was four months in 1928, when he was loaned to the Vatican Library in Rome to introduce the Library of Congress cataloging system. Upon arrival in Rome, the Americans were given a private reception by Pope Pius XI, who himself had once been a librarian. When the Pope learned that his guests spoke German, he talked very openly and cordially to them. The Vatican Library is the world's richest treasure house and is said to occupy more than 11,000 rooms!

Hanson enjoyed Rome. Since the Internationl Bibliographic Congress was to meet the following year in the Eternal City, he was asked to serve as one of 11 delegates on the planning committee. Imagine his surprise when he found out that two of the others were not only from Norway but from Valders!

One of the strange things about Hanson's story is that when Jens first arrived in America, he wrote letters to his family pleading that he be sent home to Norway "by mail." Who can guess what is in store for a child? Hanson reorganized five major libraries and is the chief author of the cataloging rules used today throughout the world. What a loss to the world would have occurred if his parents had sent him a return ticket.

CHAPTER 26

Knute Reindahl —
Violin Maker

SCANDINAVIANS HAVE BEEN VERY fond of wood carving and music. These talents met in Knute Reindahl. Born in Telemark in 1858, his father died when he was just three years old. He had come from a family of silversmiths who were always carving wood as well. On his mother's side, an uncle was considered the best rosemaler (ornamental painting) in Norway. Her name, Gulbek, was also found on the finest violins in the land. His great-grandfather was the king's bodyguard in war and was thought to be the strongest man in Norway. He used to break up feuds at wedding parties. That's how he met his death by an iron bar over his head.

When Knute was nine, his mother emigrated to Madison, Wisconsin. A boat accident in the Skien harbor made her wish she had never left. Times were tough for immigrants in America. She worked in the harvest fields and his sisters worked as hired girls. Yet he remembered these as the happiest days of his life. Knute got little schooling. He never passed beyond the fifth grade, even though he was a year older than his teacher. He'd rather carve salad bowls and picture frames than study in books. Selling his hand-made trinkets, he visited the Indian camps on Lake Monona by the city. They taught him how to make bows and arrows.

Realizing that wood carving was his chief interest, Knute returned to Norway in 1887 to study ornamental carving. He had learned that the best violin makers had originally been woodcarvers. He also tried his skiing skills in the mountains of Telemark. Trying to outjump his brother, both skis fell off and he landed like an arrow into the soft snow.

Success in America did not come quickly, but hard work and determination had its rewards. When the Chicago Symphony moved into the newly built Orchestra Hall on Michigan Avenue, the old violins built by masters were too weak to be heard. The Director bought five of Reindahl's violins in their place. In 1900, the Reindahl Violin won the

Diploma of Merit for woodcarving and had a special medal struck for it at the World's Fair in Paris. He was the only violin maker mentioned in the "Who's Who" of the World's Columbia Exposition in Chicago.

One of the dreams of a violin maker is to discover the "lost art of the masters." One of the great swindles in musical instruments is people who claim to have made this discovery. Knute contended that the only magic was good workmanship. His wood was spruce from the ruins of a 14th century stave church near Oslo. How good were his instruments? In 1922, when the city of Madison wanted to honor Fritz Kreisler, they presented him with a Reindahl Violin. Nothing less would do for the "master."

A Danish violin teacher by the name of Adamsen, who had studied in Italy, said of the Reindahl Violin: "I am surprised that anybody can make that good a violin here in America." One writer has described Reindahl as "the outstanding artist in wood among Norwegian Americans." The artist's comment about his life was: "I was always whittling." And through his hands, personality passed into his works of art.

CHAPTER 27

Anna The
Immigrant Girl

MUCH HAS BEEN WRITTEN about the men of Scandinavia who came to toil in the New World. But what about the women? The record leaves no doubt that they were just as heroic and hardworking as the men, and often outlived their husbands.

Anna Hedalen was a typical frontier woman. Born in 1841, her parents emigrated the week after she was confirmed at age 15. She had taken care of some neighbor's children and the neighbor lady wanted to keep her behind in Norway. Her mother, however, could not bear the thought of such a separation. As a token of appreciation, the neighbor gave her a lace dress for confirmation.

The first day out of Bergen, every passenger was sick except Anna and two men. She worked night and day to bring water and food to the other passengers.

The Hedalens went to a farm eight miles east of Madison, Wisconsin. In the winter of 1856-57, Anna worked as a servant in the governor's mansion. She spoke to the First Lady in "sign language" until she acquired English. Many nights she cried herself to sleep and lit a candle to read from the hymnal to forget her lonesomeness. She was glad she'd studied her confirmtion lessons faithfully, as memorizing hymns was part of the program.

Preferring farms to city life, Anna worked in the fields for five years, doing men's work. She knew how to hitch up the oxen to the "kubberulle" (wagon). Because she was gentle with them, they responded willingly.

Anna married Nils Ellestad in 1860. Neither of them had money, yet they always had something to give a neighbor in need, and the Indians who came for soup and "kaape" (coffee). If a baby was born in the neighborhood, Anna would bring a kettle of "rommegrot" (cream porridge).

Eleven children joined their home. Anna never had so much as a midwife or a doctor, nor had she seen a hospital bed. When the children were small, she'd tie the youngest on her back while milking the cows in the yard. The only problem was that when the flies were bad the cow's tail would start to swish. In the winter, when Nils was busy cutting wood, she did the milking as well as the cooking. Besides this, Anna sheared the sheep, carded the wool and spun the yarn before knitting clothes for the children. They never had store-bought clothing.

The "Yankees" who had settled before the coming of the Scandinavians always felt that they were better than the newcomers, certainly more stylish. That didn't bother Anna. It wasn't long before the natives could see that their new neighbors were cultured people and highly literate. They said: "Them 'ere Norwegians are almost as white as we are, and they kin read too, they kin." They didn't have many books, just the Bible, catechism, and a hymnal. Many homes also had an "Andagtsboker" (daily devotional book). The Ellestad dining room served as the "parochial school." This was how faith was kept alive for the immigrant families.

As they began farming, cinch bugs took their barley, wheat and corn for the first three years. Yet optimism prevailed, like the title of Bette Smith's book, "Tomorrow Will Be Better." The saving feature to Anna's charm was that even on her 92nd birthday, a visitor reported that she had not lost her sense of humor.

CHAPTER 28

Skansen —
Sweden In Miniature

I F YOU COULD VISIT just one place in Sweden, where would you go? I'd suggest Skansen, an open-air museum which covers 75 acres. Two million people a year visit Stockholm's greatest tourist attraction, twice as many people as live in Sweden's capital city.

Back in 1891 when Skansen was founded, it was on the outskirts of the city, but today it's a green and car-free oasis in the middle of the city. You get a magnificent view on all sides. The skyline is marked by copper roofs, church steeples, Sergels Tower and modern skyscrapers, plus the hills and canals.

Skansen has a little bit of every part of Sweden. It is arranged with a feeling for geography. For example, the Lapp village is placed in the northwest. The far northern part is ringed with natural habitat for the larger wild animals. Moose, bears, wolves, wolverines, lynx and even European Bison, now extinct except in captivity, live peacefully in the heart of this beautiful metropolitan area. Most of the animals are native to Sweden, but since this is Stockholm's only zoo, there are also some tropical exhibits.

Skansen was the dream of Arthur Hazelius who began collecting Swedish cultural exhibits in 1872. A practical man with an eye for education, he wanted to preserve some of the everyday life from Sweden's past. He seemed to sense that the 20th century would bring sweeping changes to his country.

With meticulous effort, Hazelius brought buildings and furnishings to Stockholm. His work has served as a model for other open-air museums throughout the world. Of special interests are the farmsteads transplanted into Skansen. In the earlier days when people could not drive to town for all of their needs, the blacksmithing, baking, cloth making and sowing had to be done on the farm. It took many buildings. The farm owners lived in the main house and the workers in others,

56

called "outhouses." Cattle were housed in buildings which joined the living quarters of people.

Of special interest is the summer farmstead, the "faabod," or "seter" in Norwegian. These were usually found in northern Sweden and were places where cattle, goats and sheep were kept in the summer. Sometimes there was a nearby summer farm and another up to 50 miles away from home. Usually these summer farms were jointly owned by 8 to 10 owners with about 25 cows. They were tended for about nine weeks in the summer by older women with the help of children. They also put up hay, and made cheese and butter.

I found only one building in Skansen that was imported. It was a "stabbur" from Telemark in Norway. The Swedes also used these houses to store dairy products and food. There is also a large "Dalarnahest" (a horse carved from wood in Dalarna) with steps for people to climb up on and have their picture taken. To have your picture taken on it is the equivalent of being photographed on a camel near the pyramids at Gizeh in Egypt.

Skanson is both an historical museum and a recreational center. There are restaurants, theatres, art exhibits and concerts. Skansen is ten times as large today as it was in 1891. The exhibits and animal habitats are constantly being improved. I spent several hours walking through it with a guide book. If you go to Stockholm, insist on visiting Skansen. It's Sweden in miniature.

Spinning wheel demonstrated at Skanson.

CHAPTER 29

Knut Haukelid —
Resistance Hero

THE STORY OF KNUT HAUKELID reads like a modern Scandinavian saga. Like so many Norwegians, his parents emigrated to America. When Knut and his twin sister, Sigrid Guri, were born, the parents went back to Norway. She became a movie actress. Their roots were at Rauland in Telemark. That's rugged mountain country.

This move was to be of critical importance to the whole free world. Knut, having the blood of Vikings, returned to America to study engineering. Then he studied in Germany. There his eyes were opened to the danger of war. He listened to Hitler's speeches and returned to Norway with disgust.

On April 9, 1940, when the Nazis attacked Norway, Knut was in Trondheim. He woke up in the morning to discover the city occupied by the enemy. Slipping into the countryside, he tried to join a fighting unit, but was unsuccessful. Norway had depended on its neutrality and was not ready for war.

Haukelid's day to serve his country came on February 28, 1943, when the British dropped him with nine other commandos on the Hardanger flats, some of the harshest winter terrain in the world. I have driven across it and have some idea of how difficult it would be to survive there in frozen snow. Stories have been written and movies have been made how they made their way by night to the Norsk Hydro Plant near Rjukan. Their mission was to destroy the plant which made heavy water (deuterium oxide). This substance would make it possible for Hitler's war machine to create a nuclear bomb. Eluding the guards, they destroyed both equipment and stores, and then escaped. The German occupation general, Nikolaus von Falkenhorst, said it was "the best coup I have ever seen."

The plant, however, was back in operation two months later. After the Americans bombed it in November, the Nazis decided to remove the equipment and heavy water stores to Germany. Informers within the plant sent word to Britain. Haukelid was given the task of preventing this transfer. Disguised as a laborer, he boarded the ship and planted 19 pounds of explosives. On Sunday morning, February 20, 1944, the ship carrying the dreaded cargo exploded and sank in the deepest part of Lake Tinnsjo. That ended Hitler's chance of getting the bomb.

The Resistance Museum in Oslo has an excellent exhibit of the hydro plant and how Haukelid and his companions did their work. If you go to Oslo, it is a "must" to see.

After the war, Haukelid became a Lt. Colonel and concentrated his energies on Norway's defense. Today, Knut and his wife, Bodil, spend their winters in Oslo and their summers at Lillesand, on the coast between Arendal and Kristiansand. He still finds time to go back to the family's mountain hotel at Rauland in northwest Telemark to hunt reindeer.

The Norsk Høstfest Association of Minot, ND, honored Haukelid by inducting him into the Scandinavian-American Hall of Fame in 1985. It was a distinct privilege for my wife and I to be his hosts when he visited Minot. I also improved my knowledge of those dark days of World War II from our visits. Having dual citizenship in the United States and Norway, he brings honor to both countries for his dedication to freedom and peace. He has to be called one of the great heroes of the twentieth century.

CHAPTER 30

The Cathedral
In Trondheim

NO CHURCH IN THE WORLD is as exciting to me as the Nidaros Cathedral in Trondheim. This is not because it is the largest church in Scandinavia, but because of the story that goes with it. I grew up with a picture of this church in the living room of our farm home.

The Nidaros Cathedral dates to July 29, 1030, the day King Olaf Haraldsson fell in the battle of Sticklestad. Olaf's body was carried 75 miles by friends from the battlefield to the River Nid for burial. Soon people began claiming that miracles were performed by the fallen king. A year later, Bishop Grimkel, declared Olaf to be a saint and martyr. His body was put in a silver casket studded with jewels and placed on the altar in Clemen's Church.

It was not long before Olaf was called "Norway's Eternal King," a title still given to him. On the sight of his burial, a spring of water began to flow and people came to it for healing, according to the saga by Snorre Sturluson. A chapel was built and the altar was placed where Olaf had been buried. Soon a flood of pilgrims from all over northern Europe began trekking to Trondheim, making it the fourth most frequented holy place on the continent.

Olaf's younger brother, King Olaf Kyrre, began building the new Christ Church on the site in 1070. Many fires have ravaged this church, but it has always been restored. The most recent renovation began in 1869. The length of the building measures almost 400 feet. The baroque organ, the largest in Scandinavia, was built in 1930.

The work of many famous sculptors adorns this building. One of these, Gustav Vigeland, is best known for his statues in Frogner Park in Oslo. The husband of a cousin to my father, Stephen Krogstad, spent his entire lifetime making statues for the west wall. He was twice honored by the King for his work.

The greatest feeling for this historic church is experienced through worship. Despite the splendid architecture and furnishings, the liturgical service is quite plain. Even if you know only a little Norwegian, it is not difficult to follow. I timed the pastor's sermon. He used only 11 minutes for the prayer, reading of scripture and the sermon. He spoke very plainly and clearly. There was nothing pompous about it. The sanctuary was fairly well filled, including quite a few young people. The music was outstanding, both the choir and the organ. Concerts and recitals are regularly held in the nave.

Whenever I approach this gray soapstone building, I get the feeling of walking on holy ground. The cathedral towers above all other buildings in the city and can easily be reached by walking from any part of the downtown. A cemetery surrounds it on the north and east.

I have been to Nidaros several times and will be drawn back to it again. Whatever a person may think about the saga accounts of Olaf the Saint, there is a mystique about this place. Even though Olaf's body has secretly been buried somewhere in or near the cathedral and the casket melted down in Denmark, Nidaros continues to cast its spell on all who visit it.

Nidaros Cathedral in Trondheim.

CHAPTER 31

Denmark's 'Jelling Stone'

I T WAS WITH GREAT EXCITEMENT that we visited Jelling (pronounced "yelling"), the "birthplace of Denmark," on a beautiful September day in 1985. I was surprised that we were the only tourists in this famous place and I told some of the local folks that if this had been in America, we'd have built a Disneyland here. They claim, however, that 150,000 people visit the Viking remains in Jelling annually.

Jelling is a small city about 12 miles northwest of Vejle ("Vai-la"), in south Jutland where Lego blocks are made. It's near the highway coming up from Germany through Jutland to the North Sea. Two large earth mounds, each with fifty steps to the top, mark the historic site. A white church stands in the middle. The mounds are two ancient Viking burial sites. One of them was built as the tomb for King Gorm (d. 960), the first king to rule over a united Denmark. The other was for his wife, Queen Thyra.

The mounds have been excavated and yielded some interesting finds. The investigation began in 1820, but no human remains were discovered. Among the objects found was a little silver goblet. Further work was continued by King Frederik VII (1846-1866), who had a special interest in archaeology.

After World War II, the ground under the church was excavated. Remains of three earlier wooden churches were found. The oldest of these is believed to have been built by Gorm's son, King Harald. It was larger than the present church and is the biggest wooden church to have been found in Scandinavia. It was a Viking Age cathedral. The skeletal remains of a man who is believed to have been King Gorm were found under the church together with gold wire and jewelry, but not a trace of Queen Thyra's remains.

The most important discoveries at Jelling, however, were two large stones with runic writing. On the smaller is written, "King Gorm made these sepulchral monuments to Thyra, his wife, the grace of Denmark." This is the earliest mention of the name "Denmark" on Danish soil. Gorm and Thyra founded the royal line that extends to the present Queen, Margrethe II. King Olav V of Norway and Queen Elizabeth II of Great Britain also trace their ancestries to this line.

The larger runestone reads: "King Harald had these sepulchral monuments made to Gorm his father and to Thyra his mother, when Harald had conquered all Denmark and Norway and made the Danes Christians." This stone has been called Denmark's "baptismal certificate." There is an image of Christ on the stone which resembles a victorious Viking king. I bought a picture of the larger stone with both the Old Norse and modern Danish translation of the runic writings. Gorm remained a heathen to the end, but Thyra accepted the Christian faith. Further mysteries remain to be solved in the Jelling discoveries.

Looking about the village, I discovered that Thyra and Harald are commemorated better than Gorm. A restaurant claims the name of Queen Thyra and a steak house is named after King Harald "Blautand" (bluetooth). Perhaps he fell off his horse and damaged a tooth. The present monarch is remembered by the Hotel Margrethe which advertises a night-club discoteque called "Hot Maggie." It seemed irreverent to this American tourist to refer to such a highly regarded queen in that manner. If you visit Denmark, try to get out into country and see the place of Denmark's baptism.

The Jelling Stone.

CHAPTER 32

Helsinki's
'Rock Church'

WHAT SHOULD CITY PLANNERS do when a huge rock formation lies in the middle of its downtown development? Blast it with dynamite or leave it? The Finns, being among the world's most creative architects, had a better idea. They designed a city square around it with one of the world's most original and beautiful churches at the center. It's called "Temppeliaukio Church."

Planning for the square began in 1906. The architectural competition for the church began in 1932, but it was not until 1961 that any plans were accepted. Two brothers, Timo and Tuomo Suomalainen, won the competition. Construction began on February 14, 1968, and it was consecrated on September 28, 1969, at a cost of 3,850,000 marks (about $1,800,000).

Quarried into bedrock, the idea was to preserve the rock formation of the area. The church is covered by a copper dome joined to the the rock by reinforced concrete beams in between which there are 180 skylights. The floor of the church is on street-level, so the altar can be seen from the street through the glass doors. The interior walls are rough and jagged. Even the drill marks have been preserved to let the working methods remain visible. The walls are from 15 to 30 feet high.

The altar consists of a slab of smoothly sawn granite. During the summer, morning sunlight falls against it during the service. The altar wall is formed by an ice-age rock crevice. A small crucifix portrays Christ as sufferer and victor. Twenty-five people can kneel for communion at a time. Wheelchairs can be brought to the altar rail.

Space is provided for radio and television broadcasting and for an orchestra. The Finns are great lovers of music. The acoustics and lighting simply overwhelm the visitor. The organ has 43 registers, 4 manuals, a pedal and 3001 pipes. A tunnel leads to a two floor parish house, which includes four clubrooms. The building is heated from the central municipal heating network and it is mechanically ventilated.

The church building serves a parish of the Evangelical Lutheran Church of Finland. Twelve thousand members are counted, an unusually large number by American standards. Over 170,000 people annually attend church functions. Concerts and recitals are also held there frequently. About a half million visitors come each year from all over the world. We were among them.

This building is such a surprise. But its ingenuity is typically Scandinavian. They disturb the landscape as little as possible during construction. The same goes for private homes. It's an architect's paradise.

We were greatly impressed by the stark simplicity and utter beauty of this church. It's an awesome feeling to sit in the pew and see the sun streaming down through the skylights. There is a feeling of spaciousness. Even when the pews are filled, you don't feel "fenced in." If you visit Helsinki, be sure to see this 20th century architectural wonder. Spend some time in the "Rock Church." It's good for both body and spirit.

CHAPTER 33

Hans Hyldbakk —
'King Of The Cliff'

"KLEIVAKONGEN," "KING OF THE CLIFF," they call him. Hans Hyldbakk is the best known person in Surnadal, my ancestral valley, 75 miles southwest of Trondheim. At 88, he was waiting for another book of poems to be published. In addition to poetry, Hyldbakk has published seven large volumes of local history called "bygdeboker."

My visit to this famous writer in September 1985 was a moment of excitement. He is the only living link between our family before the immigration and myself. After grandpa Ola (Ole) Olsen Fiske emigrated to America in 1892, great-grandmother Margrethe was left alone with her small herd of cattle and goats. During the summer, she assumed the role of a dairymaid and went up to the Fiske seter (summer pasture) in the Trollheim mountains.

In 1910, when Hans was 13, he was a "gjaetar" (literally, "goatherd") in that seter. He wrote a poem about Margrethe, describing her as the best of the dairymaids. When she served the boys cream for their bread, she dipped deep into the container to bring up the thickest and sweetest. She also darned their socks, dried their wet clothes and made their beds. They didn't forget. Margrethe lived until 1920 and never saw grandpa Ole after he emigrated to North Dakota. I just discvered this good woman a few years ago, but now her picture hangs proudly in our family room.

Hyldbakk lives in a small hytte (cottage) high above the village. To get there we had to drive through cattle gates over a switchback trail. Directing us to his home was a local journalist, Magne Holten. It was a beautifully cool morning with bright sunshine. I could see why Hans liked it up there. He had a telephone, but neither radio nor television. As we sat across the table from each other, I felt an instant comraderie with this spry and modest man who had researched the records and traced my roots back to 1520.

A few years ago, another Surnadal journalist led a movement to get the University of Oslo to give Hyldbakk an honorary doctor's degree. When learning of it, he made it clear that the degree would be refused. Instead, a bust of Hyldbakk was placed near the court house. I had my picture taken by it.

A couple of weeks after returning home, a newspaper arrived from Surnadal. There was a full page story by Holten about our visit. The headline read, "Prest med roter fra Fiske pa Surnadals-visit." (Priest with roots from Fiske on a Surnadal visit.) There was a picture of Hyldbakk standing between my wife and myself. Holten made a point of writing that my wife is "of Danish blood." Another writer advised me that Norwegians consider a man fortunate if he has a Danish wife. That makes me a success in Surnadal! To top off the trip, Hyldbakk identified some previously unknown relatives.

When taking leave of this delightful gentleman, I promised to write a story about him. He replied with a smile, "Then I'll be famous in America." Long may he live and probably will from climbing that mountain. I agree, he is the "King of the Cliff."

CHAPTER 34

Lindholm Hoje —
Viking Winter Camp In Denmark

SHEEP PEACEFULLY GRAZE over ground where once mighty Viking warriors encamped. The place overlooks Aalborg in northern Denmark where the Limfjord cuts through the Jutland peninsula. Lindholm Hoje (pronounced "Hoi-jah" and translated "heights") gives a commanding view of the area, but mystery enshrouds the rocks which form the shape of a Viking fleet.

People used to say that the gods hurled these stones from Sweden to Denmark. Over the years, blowing sand covered the stones so that they were ignored. As early as 1889, some of the stone settings were recognized, but it was not until the German occupation forces, during World War II, dug trenches in the area that the real truth about this hill top was realized.

Six years of investigations of this Viking period site were completed in 1958. It turned out to be the remains of a settlement which contained a large cemetery. Over 700 graves have been examined, most of them being cremation remains. This would indicate a pre-Christian period. Ancient artifacts were found among these burials, including bronze ornaments, glass beads, bracelets, iron knives, coins, whetstones, wooden boxes and bones of domestic animals.

Most of the stone outlines of boats are about 25-30 feet long, except for one which is about 80 feet. The earliest dating of the findings goes back to the 7th century, almost 200 years before the Viking "breakout" into the North Sea world. There is evidence that a thriving city once was located to the north of the hill. Streets, paved with wood, have been uncovered.

Who were some of these Viking heroes that walked on this hill a thousand or more years ago? There was one event of special historical interest. In about the year 1028, Knut the Great, king over both Denmark and England, assembled his fleet in the Limfjord to invade Norway. There he prepared his fighting force to drive King Olaf from power.

After some hit and run battles, Olaf fled to Russia where the Viking rulers gave him a royal welcome. When Olaf returned two years later, he met his death against Knut's forces at Sticklestad and became a "saint."

It appears from the sagas and archaeology that Lindholm Hoje was one of the best known winter quarters for the Viking warriors, and was the permanent settlement for their families in Denmark. It's well situated for protection against the hard winter winds blowing from the North Sea. Lindholm Hoje was an ideal place to observe an enemy approaching from any direction. The latest coin found on these heights was minted about 1036-39.

The Viking warriors have all left these heights, but sheep still graze there. I asked our guide who owned them. It turns out that they have been there for generations and no one claims them. Perhaps they are Vikings in disguise, waiting for the return of their golden age when they can again become warriors and plow the seas with their longboats. As I walked across these heights and touched the stones marking the burial sites, even my feet could feel the past which the sands of the sea have not entirely covered.

CHAPTER 35

The 'Primstav' —
Old Norse Calendar

I HAD TO VISIT HAAKON'S HALL (Haakonshallen), a medieval castle in Bergen, to learn why my father always planted his corn by May 15.

The most fascinating part of the visit was to see a woolen tapestry, 80 feet long and 42 inches wide. It was completed in 1961 by Sigrun Berg. Normally, it's hanging across the length of the wall where kings used to dine. But it had been taken down for cleaning and laid out over long tables, so I was able to study it with some care.

This tapestry is a "Primstav," normally made of wood and found hanging in the entrance of a home. The word probably derives from the Latin "Primatio Lunae," referring to the New Moon. This wooden calendar, also called a "clog almanac," was the way people kept track of time in the old days. There was a notch for each day.

The Primstav is laid out horizontally to show the two seasons, summer which began on April 14 along one edge of the board and winter beginning October 14 on the other. There was mid-summer day and mid-winter day, but no spring and autumn as we celebrate. When you finish one season, you just flip the board over.

Originally, the Primstav gave weather forecasts, planting and harvesting dates, pasturing dates for cattle, moving dates, to tell when fish will bite and such things as are in the Farmer's Almanac. Community life was organized around these dates. When Christianity came to Norway in the early 11th century, 37 new holidays were added to the calendar. Religious emphasis was given to the dates from nature. The Christian holy days usually remembered martyrs, the Virgin Mary, Christ or the Apostles.

Each holy day is marked by a symbol. April 14, "Summer Day," is a tree filled out with leaves, telling people to get ready for planting. It was also moving day for hired help. If it snowed on this day, it would

70

snow nine times before full summer came. October 14, "Winter Day," has a mitten, showing that winter clothes should be taken out and put in order.

The most celebrated of the summer holidays is John the Baptist's birthday, June 24. Fires are lit everywhere on hillsides on the eve of this holiday to protect people and animals against witches and evil spirits. The cows were taken to the seters ("outfarms"). If it rained, then it would be wet during harvest. The calendar symbol is a church building. August 10 was the last day for putting up hay or it would be worthless as winter fodder. By September 14 (Holy Cross Day), all crops were to be in barns for a blessing and cattle were turned loose to graze. Anyone who did not keep holy days was fined.

Some winter day when there is a snowstorm and the phone doesn't ring, I'm going to make a Primstav for my home. Maybe there is more wisdom in it than modern people imagine.

Now another of my childhood mysteries has been explained. I'm quite sure my father didn't know the origin of his beliefs that corn had to be planted by May 15 or it would not ripen. We didn't have a Primstav in our home. But he followed its advice, and our cattle and hogs always had their winter feeding.

Primstav.

CHAPTER 36

Flying With The
Scandinavian Airline System

THERE ARE MANY GOOD AIRLINES and several which travel to Scandinavia. None of them, however, is structured like the "Scandinavian Air System." SAS is a consortium owned by the Danish, Norwegian and Swedish Airlines. The parent companies are owned 50/50 by government and private shareholders.

We weren't long on the plane before we could feel the Scandinavian atmosphere. Flight announcements were made on a movie screen with pictures of Copenhagen. The predominance of blonde cabin attendants and gentle accents left no doubt that we had already entered Scandinavia, even though we were still on the runway.

Taking off at 5:30 p.m. from Chicago's O'Hare International Airport, we landed eight hours later (8:30 a.m.) in Copenhagen. Our DC-10 flight 942 covered 3850 miles at 550 MPH at an altitude of 33,000 feet. We had a clear view of Norway's west coast near Stavanger as we began our approach to Denmark. After talking with the Purser (chief steward), I was given the Flight Map with flight data posted for the passengers.

In charge of the flight to Denmark was Captain Sverre Prestbakken. Visiting with him in the cockpit, I learned that he had attended the 1985 Hallinglaget in Tacoma, Washington. I hadn't been there, but I pulled out my membership card in the Hallinglag to prove my ethnic purity. Knowing that a Halling was in control, I relaxed even more.

We hadn't been long in the air when a full course dinner was served. It left nothing to be desired except a bigger appetite. The food was prepared under the direction of Johanna and Crister Svantesson of Gotenburg, Sweden, the home city of my good friends Elon and Norah Eliasson (see Chapter 20), famous for their culinary skills in New York City. Before landing, every passenger was given a steaming-hot hand towel to freshen up for the Continental Breakfast.

On the overseas flight, headphones were distributed so that we could either listen to a choice of music or hear the sound for a movie being shown. A cart with duty-free items for sale also passed through the aisles.

SAS was founded August 1, 1946, with headquarters in Stockholm. In addition to owning an airline, it has a score of subsidiary and associated companies. One of the reasons for SAS's rapid progress is its president, Jan Carlzon. He's a gifted communicator and an innovative leader with a Master of Business Administration degree from the Stockholm School of Economics. Each year SAS serves over 10 million passengers and carries about 160,000 tons of cargo to 90 cities in 40 countries. Almost 30,000 people are employed.

The SAS lounges are delightfully comfortable at the International terminals. There we could rest, enjoy refreshments, use a desk for writing or make phone calls. Our return to Chicago gave me the clearest view I've ever had of Iceland. Every roof top was visible in Reykjavik from 31,000 feet. This flight was captained by Leif Hansen from Copenhagen. It was as smooth as glass. He invited me to the cockpit to talk about SAS and to show me the instrument panels. I was impressed. To become the captain of an SAS overseas flight takes a long career in aviation.

The modern Vikings have improved a great deal on the longships by which they traversed the sea 1000 years ago. While the old ways must have been exciting, I prefer the new ways and am ready to fly again.

The Scandinavian Air System in flight.

CHAPTER 37

'Scoop' Jackson —
Counselor To Presidents

THE SEATTLE AREA BECAME HOME to large numbers of Norwegian immigrants. Among these was Peter Greset Isaaksen from Aure, west of Trondheim, and Marine Andersen from Norfold. Little could they have realized that their futures would be joined together in the New World and that their son, Henry, would become one of its most respected statesmen.

Like so many other immigrants, Peter did not retain any of his Norwegian names. Instead, he became "Jackson." The solid Scandinavian character of honesty and stubborn determination, however, became their trademarks as they began life in western Washington.

Henry Jackson was born May 31, 1912, in Everett, where he graduated from high school in 1930. The nickname "Scoop" was given to him by a sister because she thought he resembled a comic strip character by that name who always got others to do his work for him. He received a law degree from the University of Washington in 1935. The law office, however, was too quiet for this young Norseman. In 1938, he won his first election as prosecuting attorney. In 1940, he went to Congress as a Democrat and moved into the United States Senate in 1952, despite an Eisenhower landslide. He remained in that post until his death on September 1, 1983. He never lost an election.

When the Democrats were looking for a candidate to run against Nixon in 1972, his Senate colleagues picked him as the most qualified to be president. He didn't win the nomination, but he was highly respected by Kennedy, Johnson and Nixon who often asked his advice, particularly on matters of national defense. Kennedy chose Jackson as his running mate in 1960, but yielded to pressure for Lyndon Johnson in order to get southern votes. In 1968, he was Nixon's first choice for Secretary of Defense and was also offered the Secretary of State position. After serious deliberation, he turned down both offers.

Jackson took a hard line on Communism but believed in negotiations. He used his power to persuade the Soviets to soften their treatment of Jews. The presidents could always count on his support for defense. Together with his strong Americanism, he was also fiercely proud of his Norwegian heritage and showed his concern often for the well-being of Norway. People always knew where Jackson stood on issues. He was known to say, "I guess I'm just a stubborn Norwegian."

Jackson had a soft spot in his heart for the poor. He set up a fund to buy shoes for needy schoolchildren in his hometown. The money paid to him for speeches was used to provide scholarships for college students. No one knew where the money came from until the laws required public officials to make financial disclosures. He had never even told his staff.

On June 26, 1984, President Reagen posthumously awarded Jackson the Medal of Freedom in a Rose Garden ceremony. The president praised the senator from Washington as a protector of the nation, its freedoms and values. The epithet on his gravestone reads: "If you believe in the cause of freedom, then proclaim it, live it and protect it, for humanity's future depends upon it." All Americans can be proud of this Norseman from the West Coast. The world needs more of his kind.

CHAPTER 38

Norwegian Deaconesses
Build Hospital In Chicago

MUCH HAS BEEN WRITTEN about the strong character of Norwegian women in the Viking period and during the Middle Ages. This strength continued on in the Norwegian deaconesses who came to Chicago at the turn of the century.

Chicago was a popular stopping off place for immigrants from Scandinavia. The area around Humboldt Park and Logan Square, northwest of the Loop, is dotted with churches started by these newcomers to America.

This metropolis of the Midwest had some rough and tumble sections. It was into those places with poverty, hardship and crime that a group of young women set out to build a hospital, start a school of nursing and reach out to families in need. They had a special concern for orphans, unwed mothers, the aged and drunks on skid row.

The deaconess movement began in Kaisersworth, Germany, in 1836, under Theodore Fliedner who established its famous motherhouse. Florence Nightingale learned nursing there. It became the model for the deaconess programs throughout Europe and America. Several of the leaders in Chicago came from the motherhouse in Oslo. The head of the local order was called both "Mother Superior" and "Sister Superior." The members were called "Sisters." The name "deaconess" means "one who serves." It's a work that goes back to biblical times. Many sisters became nurses, others became social workers, parish workers and some missionaries.

Having been turned out of the first Norwegian hospital built in Chicago, the sisters did not give up. They organized a society in 1896 which became a part of the United Norwegian Lutheran Church of America. Beginning in rented quarters, they opened the Norwegian Lutheran Deaconess Home and Hospital in 1902 on Leavitt Street. H. B. Kildahl was the first rector (chaplain). The hospital continued until

1969. But this was not the end. A new medical center named Lutheran General in suburban Park Ridge, one of the finest in Chicagoland, is the successor to the deaconess' work. I was a teacher at the new hospital from 1967 to 1972 and we have a daughter-in-law who graduated from the School of Nursing.

My first contact with the Chicago Deaconess Hospital was as a seminary intern at Bethel Lutheran Church near Humboldt Park in 1950-1951. I was with a group of students invited to a Halloween party. One Deaconess in particular, Sister Magdalene Klippen, was the life of the party. It was only later that I learned of her fearless courage and her compassion for the poor of the city. A Chicago Sun Times newspaper reporter wanted a story on Sister Magdalene's skid row work, but insisted on having police protection as he followed her around. The skid row residents, however, had great affection for her. She was their "angel."

Sister Ingeborg Sponland (1860-1951), born in Norway, was Superintendent of the hospital for 20 years. She spent 66 years in deaconess work and is remembered for saying, "As a deaconess, speak with your hands. Good honest work is the best sermon." Well said. These great women represented the best of the Scandinavian heritage.

Norwegian Deaconesses in Chicago.

CHAPTER 39

Discovering
Numedal

FOR YEARS, "NUMEDAL" was a place in Norway that I could not visualize, though I knew it must be there. It was important to me as the birthplace of Grandpa Hellik (1859-1931), who was born "Thoreson," but took the Scottish name "Thompson" in America.

My dream of visiting Numedal came true in September 1985. It was a beautiful morning as we drove from Oslo past Drammen on our way to Kongsberg where Jorun Teksle, the daughter of a third cousin, met us at the railway station. We followed her through the mountain valleys past the village of Lyngdal until we came to a cozy farm nestled above a valley.

Though they had never seen my wife and myself before, we were greeted as though we had always been the dearest of friends. And as you might guess, we didn't get away from the farm until we had eaten more tasty food than was good for our diets.

Besides meeting our long lost family, the most interesting part of the visit was to see a locally produced movie on the immigration to America. People of the community re-enacted the 1870s and 1880s. It fit right into the time when Grandpa Hellik emigrated to Kassen, Minnesota, in 1877. The movie showed how groups of immigrants formed their wagon trains, stopping by each farm along the way, as they travelled south to Kongsberg. There they re-grouped and got ready to for the trip to Drammen to board a ship for the long journey to the New World.

It was a late harvest in Scandinavia when we visited Numedal. Cousin Kjetal Teksle was busy combining. It was slow going because there had been so much rain and some of the heavy stand had lodged. I was impressed with the well kept farms. One of the interesting buildings is the "stabbur." It's a house built of logs set up on rocks (to keep mice from entering) where food and clothing were stored. The top floor was used for summer living quarters. Some of the stabburs are up to 500 or more years old.

It's a strange and fulfilling feeling to trace roots. You look at the faces and see the profiles and likenesses of family in America. The moment we saw Jorun, we knew she was kin. For a moment I almost thought I was looking at my sister Florence when she was in her 20s.

The church is important to these country folks. Every visitor is taken to see the church and to take a walk through the cemetery. Grave stones are pointed out. You start to feel close to people you've never seen whose names are carved in rock. Then you know that you're "home."

If you make such a trip, you should be so lucky as to meet the local historian. On our way to the farm, we stopped to see Sigurd Vinger in Flesberg. His well organized notes will some day become a "bygdebog," a regional history. He asked me to find out more about family who were missing to him because they had gone to America. I asked him how far back he could trace our roots. He said, "to about 1400." That's an awful lot of history to absorb. It's scary too, you never know what you'll find. But if the ancestors from Numedal were anything like the cousins we discovered on this trip, I'd like to meet them all.

CHAPTER 40

Trolls And
Mountain Roads

I F YOU EVER GO TO NORWAY, look out for the trolls. I've never actually seen a live one, but there's been so much talk about them that they must exist. The time to be on the alert is after dark.

I thought about this as we left Lyngdal shortly before sunset to drive to Hemsedal, north of Gol in Hallingdal. The distance isn't so far, but the roads are full of sharp curves. To save an hour of time, we crossed over the mountains at Rodberg instead of staying on the main highway through Geilo.

Saving an hour seemed like a good idea, but I had forgotten how sharp and narrow the switchback roads could be. By the time we got to Rodberg, it was pitch black. I breathed a sigh of relief when we had finally twisted our way to the top. But it wasn't over. Then we wound ourselves down until we came to a level road along the Tunnhovd Fjord. We could see farmlights along the way. I felt better by the fjord as I didn't think there'd be any trolls here.

We started to climb again as we took the fork in the road to Nesbyen. Now we were heading into troll country again. I drove carefully down the middle of the road. The last thing I wanted to do was hit one of those fearful creatures. There is no telling what kind of a spell they'd cast on us. A strange object lay on the road ahead. I slowed down, but not too slow. There it was, a large sheep sleeping on the highway. If we could get to Hallingdal and follow the river north to Gol, I figured we'd be safe. Since my earliest ancestors in America came from that valley, the trolls would probably be no danger.

After about three hours of frenzied emotions, we arrived in Hemsedal and found our motel. We hadn't seen any trolls, but we felt that they must have been watching us all the way.

If you don't believe in trolls, just read the story of the Three Billy Goats Gruff. The stories in Asbjornsen and Moe's book, "Norwegian

Folk Tales," illustrated by Werenskiold and Kittelsen, are powerful enough to convince any unbeliever.

Some people bring home troll statues when they go to Norway, but not me. I'm staying clear of them. When Paul Kemper was along on our Scandinavian tour in 1984, he showed great courage by having his picture taken alongside the figurine of an especially ugly one. I've heard that trolls try to get into people's trunks when they emigrated to America. Fortunately, so far as is known, none of them succeeded. People who claim some knowledge of these mysterious creatures say that they are ugly, have humped backs, crooked noses and wear pointed red caps. They live underground, often in fine houses of crystal and gold.

But why do trolls fascinate us humans? It's because they have magical powers, can tell fortunes and are able to make people rich, it's said. The way to scare them off is to play a stereo going full blast with rock music. They can't stand noise. Trolls don't trust anyone either, because Thor used to throw his hammer at them. They're not like the elves, called nissens in Denmark, whom farmers feed at Christmas to protect the cattle.

Ireland has its leprechauns, Germany its poltergeists, France its goblins and England its pixies. But none of them compare to the trolls for pure ugliness. Fortunately, they don't look like Norwegians. Besides that, they have tails. But my advice is, keep your eyes open!

Some friendly trolls.

CHAPTER 41

Homecoming
To Hemsedal

I T WAS 11:30 P.M. WHEN WE ARRIVED in Hemsedal, located about 150 miles northwest of Oslo. Normally it's pretty quiet in mountain villages by this time. But not on the second Monday of September when Norway elects parliament members. Just like Americans, people stay up half the night watching the returns.

It was a close battle. Unlike America, Norway has over a half dozen political parties that run hard races. When the voting is done, they make their deals to see which coalition will elect the Prime Minister. The conservative group, which included the Farmer's Party, barely squeaked through to hold power. The opposition was the liberal coalition which included the Labor Party. One of the big issues was NATO. Everyone I talked to favored staying in the alliance, but graffiti on the Oslo streets read, "NATO UT" ("NATO Out"). When the votes were counted, Norway was still in.

Unlike my other ancestral communities in Norway, we found no kin in Hemsedal. It's possible there may be some fifth cousins, but every known relative either went to America or left no heirs. One surprise is to learn how readily people changed their names a century ago. My great-grandparents from Hemsedal have Ole and Kari Bakken written on their gravestones by Walcott, North Dakota. Back in Hemsedal, they had been known as "Holle." It's not strange then that their children took different names in America. Most of them chose Johnson, except for son John who took Olson. He claimed there were too many Johnsons in the community. His mail kept getting mixed up with neighbors.

The most interesting discovery in Hemsedal was a place called "Skinnfellgaarden" ("Fleece Court") about two kilometers from the village. It's a collection of old houses from Hallingdal where Vult and Martin Simon carry on a business of making handmade clothing from lambskins. You can buy anything from a headband to a full length coat. The unique feature of their product is the "krotingene," the printing on leather with old secret symbols used in Norway about 200 to 250 years ago.

The Simons claim to be the only people who possess the secret of making dye from boiling the bark of alder or birch trees and imprinting it on leather with wooden blocks. I bought a lambskin cap in an old Norse pattern which is unusually comfortable and warm and which weighs little more than feathers. It feels pretty good in North Dakota winters. The "kroting" on my cap is the symbol for life, taken from the picture of the spinal column. It was their belief that life was in the spine. It's my guess that this is an old Viking idea derived from the fact that if a person received a blow on the back with a battle axe, life would depart. That seems likely.

In our homecoming to Hemsedal, we met no one in particular, but did catch a good view of the land of my earliest origins in America. It's a beautiful place for skiing, fishing and hiking. Ole and Kari, however, chose the prairies of the New World. I'm glad they did, but wish that mountain valley were a little closer.

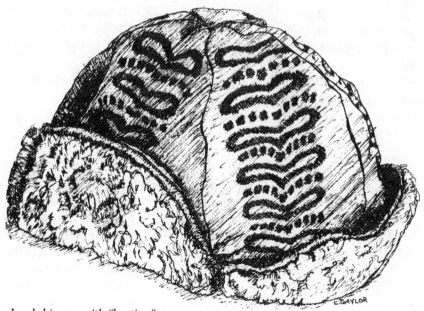

Lambskin cap with "kroting."

CHAPTER 42

The Viking
World

T HE VIKINGS WERE VICTIMS of bad press. That's because their enemies wrote so much about them. Even the name "Viking," which could often be translated "pirate," refers to to those who went "a-viking." This refers to their sailing up the bays or inlets of rivers in their shallow-draught longboats. The Viking period is from about 800 to 1066 A.D. No one is claiming that they were paragons (equal to God) or even saintly, but some of them were also expert craftsmen and did far more trading than raiding. They also had a highly developed system of democracy. Our American tradition of a free society can be traced through England back to the "Things" (assemblies of free men) of pre-Christian Norway.

No one should doubt, however, the fierceness of Viking warriors. They terrorized the North Sea lands and ravished France, Germany and Italy. Viking warriors formed the backbone of the Emperor's private guard in Constantinople during the 11th century. But for the most part, they were colonizers who quickly learned the language of the land and adopted their customs. This was especially true of the Normans (North-men) who settled in northwest France. The majority of the Vikings were farmers, merchants and craftsmen. They were the finest shipbuilders of their day.

Besides being the first to carry on regular voyages to America, the Vikings travelled the coasts of Spain, the Mediteranean and followed the camel trains into Asia along the international silk and spice routes. To Ireland they came to buy cloth and slaves. To England they came for tin, honey and wheat. In Russia, they built trade centers and dealt in furs, slaves and honey. Across France they bought wine and salt, and in Germany they obtained pottery, glass and weapons. Their early interest in Scotland was looting monasteries. Besides these, they dealt in gold, silver, jewelry, walrus ivory, hides, amber, feathers, timber, fish, ropes, soapstone and falcons.

The settlements in Iceland, Greenland and on the islands off the coast of Scotland became regular stops for the Viking summer tours. Their New World travels were known to Columbus who, it is said, went to Iceland to study maps before he took his three ships across the Atlantic in 1492.

Numerous exhibitions of the Viking world have been shown in America. One of these was at the Museum of Science and Industry in Chicago during the Spring of 1982. I was especially impressed by the gold jewelry from Birka in Sweden.

No one should suppose that Viking lifestyle was all glamor. It was a hard life trying to eke out a living in the cold northlands and risking life on stormy seas. Like modern Scandinavians, they enjoyed the warm climate and easy life of the Mediterranean. But like so many modern Scandinavians, they returned to the cooler climates of the North where their traditions and customs thrive best.

The Museum of Science and Industry in Chicago published a map of the Viking world and a book, "The Vikings and Their Predecessors." These can be ordered by writing to the museum at 57th Street and Lake Shore Drive, Chicago, IL 60637. You'll be surprised at how large a world was home to the Vikings.

CHAPTER 43

Night Voyage
To Helsinki

I T WAS A BEAUTIFUL AND SUNNY September afternoon when we boarded the Silja Line cruise ship in Stockholm for Helsinki. As the liner left the dock, we got an excellent view of Sweden's capital city. For several hours, we passed between the scenic islands which make up the archipelago.

I love to travel by sea and, except for the scarcity of time, would just as soon cross the entire ocean by surface as by air. It makes an ideal vacation.

The first thing we did after getting settled was to explore the ship from end to end and from top to bottom. There's a lot of space on a modern ocean vessel. It's not like the dinky little freighters that carried our ancestors to America. Part of the fun is just being up on deck watching the scenery and taking pictures. It's especially exciting to be on deck after dark and see the stars through a clear sky and watch the ships that pass in the night.

Cruise ships do not just transport people. They're also in the entertainment business and try to entice people to spend money in the tax-free international waters. Eating is a big part of travelling on board ship. It's important to go to the dining room early, look over the menu, and make a reservation for the time you want to eat. We noticed how other tourists were dressed so we'd know what to wear. It was definitely a dress-up occasion. We asked the headwaiter for a table in the fore part of the dining room by a window so we could watch the islands as the sun set.

We were joined at our table by a couple from Finland who were Swedish by ethnic background. They were in the export business and traded with both the East and West. I learned a good deal from them and realized that our American views on politics and trade are not shared by everyone. In fact, I was impressed how well they had thought through their ideas. They appeared well informed. They liked President

Reagen's foreign policy of standing up to the Russians, even though they obviously benefited from trading with their eastern neighbors. The Finnish currency, called the "mark," is growing stronger.

We were fortunate enough to have a stateroom on the outer side of the ship. What did we like best about the trip? I think it was the restfulness of the ride, just a gentle rocking and the vibration of the diesel engines. It makes for good sleeping, though cruise ship beds are none too large.

In the morning, everybody scurried to get repacked, cleaned up and to the dining room for a smorgasbord breakfast. The Silja Liner menu was a delight, featuring a wide variety of the best Scandinavian foods. We especially like Finnish breads and think they're some of the best in the world.

As we approached the Helsinki harbor, the Finnish flag flew aloft an old fortress which once guarded the city's entrance. Dominating the skyline is the "Great Church," the Helsinki Cathedral, with its huge dome. Finally, we had arrived, ready for a new day when we would make new friends and see things we had never seen before. The shining sun proved a good omen.

CHAPTER 44

The American
Church In Oslo

A FTER WORLD WAR II, Norwegian-Americans sent money to Norway to rebuild and repair churches that had been destroyed during the war. It was also decided to build a church for an English speaking congregation as a "living monument" to remember the bond between the two nations.

"Look to the rock from which you were hewn" was the rallying cry in America as money was raised for the project. The words of Isaiah 51 were effective and on Oct. 12, 1958, Rev. Oscar C. Hanson of Minneapolis held the first service in rented space. The following Spring, on April 23, 1959, a group of 83 Americans and Norwegians formed a congregation called "The American Lutheran Church in Oslo." It has become a spiritual home for people from all over the world. Church officials and dignitaries from both government and church in Norway attended.

The idea was first formulated in 1948 by Dr. Philip Dybvig, Director of Home Missions for the Evangelical Lutheran Church, a denomination with Norse roots. It took until 1956, however, before formal authorization was given at a church convention in Minneapolis. Pastor Hanson remained until 1960. Other pastors to serve the congregation were Dr. George Aus, a seminary professor from St. Paul (1960-62); Rev. Myrus Knutson of Los Angeles (1962-68); Rev. Arnold Nelson of Milwaukee (1967-1974); Rev. James Long of Houston (1974-1979); and the present pastor, Rev. Harry Cleven from Minnesota, who has been there since 1979.

A stately new building was dedicated on Oct. 11, 1964, at 17 Fritznersgate, near the entrance to Frogner Park, famous for its Vigeland sculptures. It was designed by the Sovik, Mathre and Mattson architectural firm of Northfield, Minnesota. The King's Guard trumpeters participated in the service. The Norwegian State Church has always been cordial to the congregation. It's an easy walk from the City Hall to the church.

We had our first look at the church in June 1977, but had to wait until September 1985 for an opportunity to be there on a Sunday morning. The service was preceded by Sunday School and an Adult Forum. I sensed a great deal of excitement by the members of their congregation. Following the service, almost everyone stayed to visit.

The most striking feature on the outside of the building is a large statue of "Christ the King" mounted on the wall. Designed by Egon Weiner of the Chicago Art Institute, it was dedicated by His Majesty King Olav V on August 27, 1967. The stained glass windows also add much to the building's beauty.

Some church members are permanent residents of Oslo, but many are transitory people attached to the NATO offices, embassies, and business firms. The new Lutheran Book of Worship used in America was introduced in 1980 by Dr. Sidney Rand, United States Ambassador to Norway, who had been president of St. Olaf College. Mrs. Rand was organist for the congregation.

If you are ever in Oslo on a Sunday morning, by all means visit this friendly congregation and join them for worship and "remember the rock from which you were hewn."

CHAPTER 45

Kaare
Of Gryting

I HAD PAID LITTLE ATTENTION to "Kaare of Gryting" ("gritting") when I first read Snorre Sturluson's "Sagas of the Norse Kings." It wasn't until I visited my cousin, Kaare Rogstad in Orkdal, that I became interested in this little known king. Cousin Kaare, the "sogneprest" (head pastor) of the valley, showed me a Viking pillar with an historical marker by his parsonage that remembers a battle fought over a 1000 years ago. It took place on the fields behind the farm buildings owned by the church.

When I got back from Norway, I took another look at what Snorre had written. It so happened that another Norwegian king, Harald, decided to add to his harem a beautiful and proud young princess named Gyda. She sent word to Harald that she would not even be "honorably" married to him unless he were king over all Norway and not just a few counties. Up to that time Norway had many kings at the same time, each ruling over a small area.

The refusal of the young maiden challenged Harald and he made a vow to the pagan gods that he would not cut his hair until he had brought all Norway under his rule. One of the first places he attacked was Orkdal where Kaare of Gryting was king. Most of the Orkdal soldiers were killed, but he spared Kaare on condition that he would serve Harald. This seemed better to Kaare than death.

It took Harald ten years to fulfill his vow and his hair was pretty long when he went to the barber for a trim, after which the barber called him "Haarfager" (fine hair). That was a safe thing to say. Harald established the Norwegian dynasty which still lives in the present king, Olav V.

Harald appointed Kaare an "enforcer" to collect taxes. It turned out very profitable for him and he became an even more important man than he had been before.

Snorre tells of how Kaare of Gryting opposed the effort of King

Haakon the "Good" to make Norway Christian. He was one of eight men who vowed to root out Christianity in Norway and to force the king to sacrifice to the gods.

Years later, when King Olaf Trygvesson forced Christianity on Norway, Kaare was still a power in the community. Olaf threatened to sacrifice him along with some of other leaders to the gods "for peace and for a fruitful season." The result was that all of them consented to be baptized into the Christian faith. The pagan gods had few martyrs. From Orkdal, King Olaf went to Trondheim where he smashed the image of Thor and offered the farmers the choice of conversion or battle. They chose baptism and Olaf took many of their sons as hostages so that they would not relapse into paganism.

The old name of the present parsonage in which cousin Kaare lives is called "Gryting." It's a peaceful place today and has some good farming land around it. The present Kaare of Gryting is a very gentle man and is highly respected in that part of Norway, serving as the "Prosti" or Dean of the pastors.

The days of conflict between the old gods and the "White Christ" are long past, but not forgotten. The record is written in stone.

CHAPTER 46

The Icebreaker
'Fram'

ACROSS THE ROAD FROM the farm where I grew up in Richland County, North Dakota, there is a township called Nanson. We farmed some of that land. Later, I doscovered that it was named after a famous Norwegian, Fridtjof Nansen ("-sen" endings were often changed to "-son" in America). Nansen became world famous for Arctic explorations and for the icebreaker which he designed. On my first visit to Norway, I saw the ship now on permanent display near the Kon-Tiki Museum at Bygdoy Park in Oslo.

When Nansen went to London in 1892 to present his plans for Arctic exploration to the Royal Geographical Society, his plan was deemed doomed to disaster. But Nansen was a true scientist with a Nordic understanding of the polar regions. His ship was 128 feet long and 36 feet at its widest. The layers of planking were between 24 and 28 inches thick, with the spaces between filled with pitch to make it watertight. The bottom was almost flat. The height of the mainmast was 80 feet and the crow's nest was 102 feet above the waterline. It had a three cylinder engine capable of seven knots in calm water. The ship was named the "Fram," which means "Forward," a fit description of Nansen's spirit.

Nansen said good-byes to his wife and daughter on June 23, 1893, and sailed out of the Oslo harbor around Norway's west coast. The commander was Otto Sverdrup from a well known Norwegian family who was also a scientist. There was a crew of 12. Wherever they stopped, they were given farewell parties. On July 21, they left the coast of Norway. Stopping at islands, they hunted for meat. By mid-August, they encountered storms and by October 1 they were sitting on ice. Polar bears visited them several times. One came on board and killed some of the dogs.

During the winter, there was nothing to do but wait until spring. The snow storms were fierce, long and cold, down to minus 56 degrees.

Despite their situation, they celebrated Christmas with a gourmet dinner, including fish pudding and cloudberries. The 17th of May (Constitution Day) was greeted with outbursts of patriotism. The Fram sailed all summer and went 2000 miles east of Norway on the north coast of Siberia before it began its return trek. On March 14, 1895, Nansen and Lt. Frederick Johansen left the Fram by dog sled for the polar cap. On April 7, 1895, they stopped, 226 miles from their goal, but 200 miles closer than anyone had ever been. They could go no further. After a perilous journey by sled and kayak, Nansen returned to Norway in mid August. All his dogs had had to be killed. A few days later, Sverdrup arrived with the Fram. The expedition was hailed as a great scientific success. Oxford and Cambridge gave honrary degrees to Nansen, then 34 years old.

Nansen did not return to the Arctic, but served his country well through teaching and statecraft. He had become the most famous man in all Norway. What were his future conquests? That remains for another story. But if you go to Oslo, see the Fram for yourself. It still looks like a grand ship.

CHAPTER 47

The Promise
Of America

AMERICA HAS BEEN THE DREAM of many people. Scandinavians may have been the first Europeans to arrive, but they were slow to follow the voyages of Columbus. Many individual Norsemen came in pre-Revolutionary days, but only the Swedes along the Delaware River formed a colony (1638).

Not until after the wars of Napoleon did the Scandinavians look to America as a "land of promise." It began with the "Sloopers" who sailed on the Restauration from Bergen in 1825. Letters reached the homeland and soon "America Fever" spread like wildfire. (See chapters 51-53.)

The Norwegian immigration has been carefully documented and made into an exhibit entitled "The Promise of America," first displayed in Oslo in 1984. We visited it and were highly impressed. Beginning in June 1985, the exhibit was at the Minnesota Historical Society, next to the State Capitol, in St. Paul for a whole year. It attracted thousands of visitors.

Prof. Odd S. Lovoll of St. Olaf College in Northfield, MN, has written a book entitled "The Promise of America: A History of the Norwegian-American People," published by the University of Minnesota Press (1984). It's a magnificent volume telling the story of the immigration days (1825-1925) and has some fascinating pictures. The book was sent to all members of the Norwegian-American Historical Association.

What was the "promise" of America? To be sure, many stories that reached Norway were greatly exaggerated. But can you imagine how a landless young Norwegian felt when he came to America and claimed 160 acres of black soil, often free of rocks? That enabled him to ignore the obstacles: Grasshoppers, prairie fires, rattlesnakes, three day blizzards, droughts, sod shanties, "Savages" and long distances to market. It was worth the risk. In America, the peasant boy didn't even have to take off his hat for the sheriff or the pastor!

Wisconsin became the first center of "New Norway," followed by Iowa, Minnesota, the Dakotas, Montana and the Pacific Northwest. Brooklyn, Chicago, Minneapolis and Seattle still have large Norwegian populations. Pastors, both ordained and lay, travelled tirelessly to every community where their fellow countrymen were living. They built academies and colleges which became famous for their excellence, because they didn't want their children to be "second class" citizens. They were forever reading. Their newspapers and publishing houses flourished. Augsburg Publishing House in Minneapolis has become one of the largest in our land.

They started ethnic organizations which are still growing today. Politics and debating were in their blood. They became governors, senators, Supreme Court justices and vice presidents. Fierce patriotism has been their trademark. Today only a few speak the mother tongue, but most still hold deep feelings in their hearts for their ethnic homeland. At no time did I see this more vividly than in 1983 when Norway's Princes Astrid visited the Norsk Høstfest in Minot, ND. There were no dry eyes in the audience as they sang, "Ja, vi elsker dette landet" ("Yes, We Love that Land"). Would they return? Most would say, "only for a visit." They still believe in the "promise of America."

CHAPTER 48

The Hans Christian
Andersen House

EVERY VISITOR TO DENMARK should include a trip to Odense on the island of Fyn, the home of Hans Christian Andersen. He's the best known Dane in the world and one of the most famous story tellers of all time. To get there, take a bus or rent a car in Copenhagen and cross the "Store Belt," a sound which separates the islands Fyn and Sjaelland (Zealand). It's a lovely two hour ride on the ferry.

The museum which houses his writings and the story of his life is a modest building for so famous a man, but it is laid out well and is a fascinating place to visit.

The museum ("Hus"), believed to be the place where Andersen was born, was founded in 1905, 100 years after his birth. Because so many artifacts have been gathered, it's been necessary to enlarge the building twice. It houses both library and archives. For those who want to do research on his life, this place is a "must." Original manuscripts of his writings are on display. I was especially interested in "The Emperor's New Clothes" with its corrections written in ink.

The museum follows a chronology of Andersen's life. His baptism and confirmation certificates are hung on the walls, as well as letters, report cards and the story of how he went to Copenhagen and became a great writer.

In one room, the visitor can use cassettes and headphones to listen to his stories being retold in several languages by distinguished actors. Every known publication of his work in both Danish and in translation is found on the book shelves. It's like reading his own autobiography, "The Fairy Tale of My Life."

That story takes place in a little house with three tiny apartments a few blocks away where Andersen lived from age two to fourteen. His father was a shoemaker and they, like all their neighbors, were poor.

The large domed hall in the museum has paintings which cover the walls and tell the story of his life.

Andersen was also a visual artist. He was forever drawing pictures and making paper-cuts. Some of these are in the museum and they show many facets of his great imagination. Children loved watching him use scissors while he made paper-cuts in his later years. Here his ability to fantasize has rarely been equalled. One of these is a "sun face" which has been reproduced in extra large size and hangs above the entrance to the museum. He was at his best when entertaining children.

Andersen did not own a house. He preferred to live with friends or stay in a hotel. The museum has a room furnished with period furniture to show his study where he lived during his last years (1871-1875).

Two famous statues of Andersen have been erected in Denmark. One of these is in nearby Hans Christian Andersen Gardens on the banks of the Odense river by St. Knut's cathedral. The other is in the King's Gardens in Copenhagen, across from the entrance to Tivoli Gardens.

As far as I can learn, Andersen was not overly anxious about money. He grew up in poverty. His wealth was in the stories which he gave to the world. They continue to excite and enrich both young and old.

Home of Hans Christian Andersen.

CHAPTER 49

Stockholm's
'Gamla Stan'

ONE OF THE QUAINT PLACES to visit in Scandinavia is "Gamla Stan" (Old Town) in Stockholm, Sweden. It's built up around the royal palace. A fortification was erected there about 1150 for the city's defense. The present palace was completed in 1760. It's now a museum open to visitors. The royal family has chosen to live where they have more privacy.

Sixty-eight places of interest are pointed out to visitors on this peninsula connected with bridges to the city's main shopping area to the north. It contains some of the most interesting old buildings in Sweden. Many have been restored and are used for businesses. We stayed in the Reisen Hotel along the east edge of Gamla Stan which overlooks the waterway that connects with the Baltic Sea. Through the hotel window, we saw ocean liners coming in to dock and ferries transporting people to their homes on the many islands which make up the metropolitan area of Sweden's capital city. On a nice day, sailboats are cutting the waves.

We went on a walking tour through Gamla Stan. Next to the palace was the Storkyrkan (Cathedral) with its famous statue of St. George and the Dragon, a favorite mythology of Scandinavia. As we passed the German Church, we visited wih a man coming out from the fenced enclosure. Stockholm has had a large German community since 1600. German is the second language for many of the city's inhabitants. It's no secret that during World War I the Swedish king favored his German wife's homeland. The royal family, however, detested Hitler and gave whatever help they could to both Denmark and Norway. There is also a Finnish Church just south of the Cathedral. Finland was ruled by Sweden for about 600 years and travel between the lands is still common.

A few blocks to the west is Riddar Holmen, an island that is now connected to Gamla Stan. In the 13th century, it was the home of Franciscan

98

monks who built a cloister. One of the famous names in Stockholm and on this island is Birger Jarl who founded the city. His statue was erected in 1854 and occupies a commanding position.

It's a good idea to have your camera handy when you visit these historic sites. Not only are there many unusual examples of architecture, but you can get a good history lesson just from seeing the statues which seem to be everywhere. This is particularly true in Stockholm because there hasn't been a military battle in the city for over 460 years.

Gamla Stan has a variety of small shops which are international in character. The Swedish crown had been devalued when we there in 1985 so that American money went a long way. We also got our money's worth because Swedish craftmanship is famous for its quality, especially crystal, furs, woolen clothing and steel products. I usually look for book stores and I was not disappointed.

It's a wonder that this area has been so well preserved. Fires have destroyed many of the original buildings. But the Swedes are proud of their past and have spent the money necessary to rebuild historical sites. If you want to see the best of Old Sweden, a visit to Gamla Stan alone is worth the trip to this great and beautiful country.

CHAPTER 50

Bindslev —
A Small Town In Denmark

I T'S A VILLAGE UNKNOWN to most tourists, even to those who visit Denmark. Bindslev (Binsloo) is located four miles from the sand dunes of the North Sea on Denmark's north coast and about 25 miles southwest of Skagen, the northernmost point of Europe's oldest kingdom. Nearby cities are Hjorring, Fredrikshavn and Aalborg.

My first visit to this quaint place was in 1977. My wife, Gerda, had been there before World War II to visit her grandparents and cousins. Denmark has been continually inhabited for almost 8000 years. Bindslev became an organized community for about 500 years. Today it has 1200 inhabitants. Life was a struggle here in ancient times. Today it is peaceful and cozy. The only interruption to this in recent years was during World War II when 300 German soldiers were stationed in Bindslev to operate the concrete bunkers by the seashore. Now German tourists return every summer in large numbers to vacation on the beaches.

Sixty-four businesses are listed in the "Velkommen til Bindslev" (Welcome to Bindslev) brochure. It takes only a couple of hours to walk around most of the town which is surrounded by farms. Agriculture is the most important industry. I notice two main differences between Denmark and America. The Danes plant their fields right up to the roads. No land is wasted and there are no unsightly junk yards. Denmark is like a doll's house, tidy, neat and clean.

Every Danish village has a "fotballbane" (soccer field). It's the favorite sport of the land. They also do a lot of walking. Pathways are maintained through the coulees and along the river for hikers. Bicycle paths are built along the highways. One of my hopes is to take a bicycle trip across Denmark some summer. Hostels provide rooms at a modest cost.

Like so many cities of Europe, church buildings are points of interest. The church in Bindslev (Lutheran State Church) preserves an architectural style of Denmark from the Middle Ages. The interior walls were originally decorated with Byzantine paintings, usually centered around the Madonna and Child. With the coming of the Reformation in 1536, these murals were covered with whitewash. While it hid them for hundreds of years, it also preserved them until the coating was removed in 1888.

One of my favorite places in Bindslev is Sundbaeks Bageri (bakery). It's an easy walk from any place in town to buy fresh bakery goods for breakfast, especially "rundstykker," a hard roll (not to mention the variety of genuine "Danish" sweet rolls). If you go into one of these bakeries, don't be surprised to see bees under the counter. Danes don't seem to mind them at all. In fact, it proves the quality of the product.

Our hosts in Bindslev, Erik and Betty Waehrens, lived for a while after World War II in Racine, Wisconsin. Despite the greater opportunities in America, they returned to their small town by the North Sea where they have lived "happily ever after." Every summer they entertain guests from the New World. "Deilig Danmark" (delightful Denmark) continues to charm its visitors.

The Bindslev Church.

CHAPTER 51

Cleng Peerson's
Boyhood In Norway

H E IS REMEMBERED AS Cleng Peerson, the man who began the migration of 800,000 Norwegians to America. His real name was Kleng Pedersen Hesthammer, born May 17, 1782, in Tysvaer, not far from Stavanger on Norway's southwest coast.

I always like to know what went into the child who becomes a famous person. Cleng came from Rogaland, the part of Norway where Viking expeditions were launched. These were the men who discovered Greenland and Vinland. They were born to be pathfinders.

Peersons's first 40 years were spent close to his home. Daily meals usually consisted of flatbread, herring and a bowl of sour milk. I remember how this was standard fare for many Norwegian immigrants when I was a young boy.

Cleng displayed Viking courage and stubborness while still a child. One day his father ordered him to go out into the woods to fetch his lamb so it could be butchered. Instead, Cleng went into the woodshed, placed his hand on the chopping block, and cut off the little finger of his left hand. Then he carried it to his father and placing it on a piece of flatbread, said "Here's a piece of meat for you, Father." The lamb was spared.

The Hesthammer farm was a part of the "prestegaard" (pastor's farm). When Cleng was 12, the pastor's farmhand came to claim the rent that was due. It was to be paid in flatbread. Since that year had seen a poor harvest, it meant that nearly all the food stored in their attic would have to be surrendered. His father burned with bitter anger as he cursed both the bread and the pastor. Cleng was ordered to hold the flatbread as it was delivered to the parsonage. As they crossed a bridge, he hurled it into the river below. The penalty was an extra year of confirmation instruction.

Cleng's mother was the daughter of a former pastor in the parish and she had married his father against the will of her family. His father became melancholy and spent the last years of his life in mental depression. She bore her burden with stately dignity.

Some of the religious practices of the Middle Ages remained in the valleys of Norway in those days despite the reforms of the 16th century. There was an old legend that a blind man had been healed by touching a crucifix in one of the country churches. Cleng brought a young girl who was dumb to the church so she could regain her speech. It was to no avail.

Cleng had a questioning mind, especially about religion. He found the restrictions of the state church to be painful and later became a "dissenter." During the Napoleonic wars, he was imprisoned on·board ship by the British and came in contact with Quaker missionaries. He never became one of them, but this contact provided the background for his decision to leave Norway for the freedom of the New World. Before leaving home, his mother cautioned: "There are two things that I must ask of you now that you are going away: That you guard against excessive drinking and that you shun frivolous women." She is not the only mother who has given that advice.

Cleng Peerson's boyhood home.

CHAPTER 52

Cleng Peerson Sails
The 'Restauration'

W HEN THE WARS OF Napoleon ended in 1814, Norway adopted a constitution and came under the rule of Karl Johan, king of Sweden. Times were hard due to the British blockade and there was much hunger and starvation. It was even worse for the "dissenters" who had run afoul of the State Church. Among these were some prisoners of war who had returned from England with Quaker sympathies and the followers of Hans Nielsen Hauge who preached a religious awakening in the land.

Peerson became neither Quaker nor Haugean, but he shared their dissatisfaction with the state control over religious practices, including baptisms, confirmations, marriages and funerals. He made his first visit to America in the fall of 1821 and found land for a future home for his countrymen on the shores of Lake Ontario.

Having returned to Norway, Cleng campaigned to get people interested in the New World. Many people called him a liar, but he persisted. Together with Johannes Stene, he bought a 23 year old sloop which had been used for hauling herring to Denmark and bringing grain back to Norway. Originally named "Emanuel" after the builder's son, it was later changed to "Haabet," which means "The Hope."

Before the boat was purchased, it had been renamed the "Restauration," because it had been remodelled. The sloop was 54 feet long, 16 feet wide and registered to carry 37 tons. Despite the smallness of the deck, dances were held on board.

There were two ways to America. The northern route was the most common, but ran the danger of icebergs and severe storms. The longer route was via Madiera and the Bahamas. Peerson chose the latter, despite the risks of pirates and Turkish slave traders. Setting sail on July 4th or 5th, 1825, with 6300 pounds of rod iron, there were 54 passengers, including 20 children.

104

As they approached Madiera, the pilgrims suffered from lack of drinking water. And as luck would have it, a cask of the famed Madiera wine came floating on the ocean. Though they were temperate people, in their thirst they consumed the whole barrel and as the ship sailed into the harbor, they were all asleep on the deck. At a later reception in their honor, they were the only teetotalers at the party. They learned their lesson well. Pirates were eluded by painting their hands and faces as though they had bubonic plague. While stretching out their hands and crying for help, the pirate ships quickly fled.

The "Sloopers" arrived in New York, a city of 15,000, on October 9, only to discover they were overloaded and fined $4500. Authorities impounded the ship and imprisoned the captain. It took the help of Quaker friends and an acquittal signed by President John Quincy Adams to get them out of that scrape. The ship was sold to raise money for the colony.

In October 1975, Norwegians gathered all over America to celebrate the "Sesquicentennial" (150 years) of that famous voyage which began their emigration. As a result of this celebration, several annual "fests" were begun which still meet. Among these are the Nordland Fest in Sioux Falls, South Dakota, and the Høstfest in Minot, North Dakota. A scale model of the Restauration is on display in Christ Lutheran Church in Minot. It's worth seeing.

The
"Restauration."

CHAPTER 53

Cleng Peerson's
Adventures In America

WHAT MAKES PEOPLE so restless that they set out to discover new worlds? Sometimes they just don't fit into the world where they were born. This seems to have been the case with Cleng Peerson when he led the "Restauration" expedition at age 43.

He had been married twice, but neither wife was a partner in his pioneering work. He was "tricked" into his first marriage in Norway by a much older woman of unscrupulous morals and wealth. As soon as the vows were pronounced, he fled from the scene and received no financial benefit from it. His second marriage, to a girl much younger than himself, took place in the Bishop Hill Colony of Illinois. It was a mass ceremony performed by Erik Janson from Sweden, a self proclaimed prophet, priest and king. Like Jim Jones, he came to a bad end, shot by a posse while celebrating the eucharist. The marriage ended tragically in a cholera epidemic.

Peerson's adventures in America covered three states: New York, Illinois and Texas. The first settlement in 1825 was at Kendall, on the shores of Lake Ontario, in New York. It did not turn out to be the "promised land" as they had hoped. In 1833, Cleng led an expedition to the Fox River near LaSalle, Illinois. This grew into a permanent colony of Norwegians which still exists. He is remembered as the founder of the settlement.

Of all the places in which Peerson settled, he liked Texas the best. At age 74, Cleng sold his farm in the Fox River Valley and moved to Bosque County west of Clifton in 1856. There Norwegians founded Clifton College which is now merged with Texas Lutheran College in Seguin. He loved the warmer climate of the Lone Star State. The Texas legislature awarded him 320 acres for bringing new settlers. The community is still known as Norway and was visited by King Olav V in 1981.

The war between the states was a strain on Norwegian immigrants, especially those who lived in the South. Texas was a slave-holding state. Most Norsemen were violently opposed to slavery, though it is known that a few joined the practice. His countrymen fought on both sides and some of them ended up at Andersonville, a notorious prison camp in Georgia, a place of almost certain death. Peerson also came to know the Indians well, especially Chief Shabonna who was something of a "medicine man."

In his last years, Peerson lived in a small house on the farm which he had sold to a nephew. He used to go visiting a lot. When he arrived at a farm, people stopped working to hear him tell stories, just as if it were a Sunday afternoon. His favorite food on these visits was flatbread and sour milk. He died December 16, 1865, at the age of 83. The inscription on his tombstone reads: "Cleng Peerson, the first Norwegian immigrant to America." It concludes: "Grateful countrymen in Texas erected this monument to his memory." They are not the only ones who are grateful. I join the children of 800,000 more immigrants who say, "thanks" to Cleng Peerson, the "Father of Norwegian Immigration" to America.

CHAPTER 54

The 'Great Church' In Helsinki

ONE OF THE CLEANEST CITIES that you can ever visit is Helsinki, the capital of Finland. If you enter by sea, the most commanding building to rise before your eyes is the national cathedral (Lutheran) called "Suur Kirkko" or "Great Church." It's an imposing stucture that dominates the view.

Completed in 1852, the cathedral is of neoclassic design with Russian influence. In front stands a large statue of Czar Alexander II who ruled Russia from 1855 to 1881. Erected in 1863, the statue is the work of Walter Runeberg, a famous Finnish sculptor. Finland had been under Swedish rule from 1362 to 1808 when it was seized by Russia, part of a deal made by England to secure Russia's help to fight against Napoleon. For political purposes, the government offices were moved from Turku to Helsinki, a location much closer to St. Petersburg, now Leningrad, then Russia's capital. Turku had strong Swedish influence.

Helsinki was founded in 1550 by the Swedish king, Gustav Vasa, but had suffered severely from fires. It was rebuilt during the Russian period in elegant design with wide streets and a central marketplace. Since the Czars were Christian and the head of the Russian Orthodox Church, they also gave a favorable position to the Lutheran Church. The first Orthodox Church, Holy Trinity, was built in 1827. The Orthodox cathedral was built in 1868. Both the Orthodox (1.2%) and Lutheran Churches (91.5%) receive support from the government.

The cathedral, designed by C. L. Engel, was originally called St. Nicolas' Church and is located in the famed Senate Square. It is one of several buildings constructed in the neoclassic design. The others being the University and the Government Palace. Six huge columns stand across the main entrance. A monumental set of stairs (I counted 50 steps) is laid out across the entire front of the building. This is a challenge to climb.

Once in the church, the effort is worth it. The interior is filled with light. The church is built in the shape of a cross. The altar stands in one of the transcepts with the pulpit on an inside corner of the nave. The preacher has to look at three imposing statues. At one corner is Michael Agrocola who studied theology at Wittenberg with Martin Luther and Philip Melancthon. Agricola returned to Finland and helped to effect the Protestant Reformation. At the other corners stand Luther and Melanchton. A massive pipe organ covers an entire wall. The acoustics and lighting are impressive and different from the dimly lit cathedrals built in the Middle Ages. The cathedral was the site of the Lutheran World Federation Assembly in 1963.

Helsinki was the last European city to be built as a work of art. It stands in contrast to many of the other cities of Europe with their narrow and crooked streets. The Finns are justly proud of their architectural achievements with their simple lines. Alvar Aalto has been acclaimed as Finland's most influential architect.

Among the other things to see in Helsinki is Finlandia Hall used for internatonal meetings, conventions, concerts and the performing arts. President Reagen gave an address in this hall en route to Moscow to see Prime Minister Gorbachev in June 1988. Close by is the Jean Sibelius monument, honoring Finland's most famous musician. Kaivopuisto Park with its sidewalk cafes, restaurants and open air concert area is located in the diplomatic section near the foreign embassies and consulates. But wherever you go in Helsinki, the "Great Church" stands out most of all.

CHAPTER 55

Molde —
The 'City Of Roses'

I T WAS ON AN AUGUST MONDAY afternoon when we arrived in Molde, the "City of Roses," on Norway's west coast. This community of 21,000 people barely survived the ravages of World War II. All but a few scattered houses in the center of the city were destroyed.

The Allied forces were undefeated when the British and French evacuated their forces for the defense of their own homelands. Enemy aircraft struck day and night to destroy Norway's struggling army at the end of April 1940. King Haakon VII barely escaped from Molde on the British cruiser Glasgow amidst burning docks and buildings. The Norwegian troops were left behind without weapons or supplies to hide in the countryside or be captured. This is still a sore spot in the memory of Norway's Resistance fighters. They felt betrayed by their allies. By May 1, the fighting was all over.

Today Molde is a peaceful place, having been rebuilt into a beautiful and modern city. It's located in one of Norway's most scenic tourist areas. I enjoyed walking down to the docks and watching the huge luxury liners come into port as they travel between Oslo and North Cape above the Arctic Circle. Some day, I'd like to get on one of these boats and visit all the coastal cities. Molde, however, is in an area with beauty uncommon even in a country which is famed for its scenery. Roses have been planted to help forget the war years and they grow everywhere to gild this lily of the North.

We were fortunate. Ocean clouds often roll in to darken the skies of Central Norway, but we saw the region in bright sunshine. The air felt clean, as if it were filtered. Out in the surrounding countryside of fjords and mountains is an unspoiled vacation land enjoyed in both summer and winter. Hiking and skiing are popular pastimes especially in these parts. Off in the distance, the snow covered mountains glisten whenever the sun shines. You can spend a whole day in one spot and have a change in the scenery every few minutes as the sun circles around the horizon.

The Town Hall, with its copper facade, stands in the center of Molde. There you will see a statue of the Flower Girl with her basket filled with roses. The Romsdal Fellesbank (commumity bank) stands at the main corner of the business district, covered with ivy. Nearby is the Veoy Church which stands as a symbol of faith in the heart of the community.

An annual jazz festival is held in the summer. Folk dancers come to perform for large crowds. Besides these, theatrical productions, music, art and a large selection of sporting and recreational activities make Molde a virtual paradise.

Sailboats in the bay make a beautiful picture. There is also a Fisheries Museum. Visitors can get a vivid impression of the difficult life of the coastal fishermen. Fishing boats are displayed which once provided the catch for Norway's large export of fish.

If you travel in this area, be prepared to use the ferry boats. Each county runs its own transport system. They operate efficiently and on time, with the aid of government subsidy.

Molde is about 150 miles southwest of Trondheim, the main Norwegian city north of Oslo, and about 40 miles south of Kristiansund. About 20 miles north is the village of Farstad. This had special interest to my friend Idar Farstad of Minot who was on our tour. Cousins met him in Molde and took him to see his father's birthplace.

If you go to Molde and don't have relatives to host you, I recommend eating at the Alexandra Hotel. Better food you can hardly find. But don't be in too big a hurry to move on, stop to smell the roses.

CHAPTER 56

The 'Independent Order of Vikings'

SCANDINAVIANS HAVE BEEN COMING to America since the days of Leif Erikson. But up until the war between the states, most of them melted into the English speaking world. After the war, when they came in large numbers and formed strong ethnic communities, they began to organize into fraternal groups to preserve their Old World values.

Eleven immigrants of Swedish descent organized the "Independent Order of Vikings" in Chicago on June 2, 1890. They had as their goals: "Unity of fellowship, help in time of need, and a sound investment in the future." Though founded by Swedes, who still make up the largest part of the membership, since 1951 all Scandinavians and spouses have been welcomed into its fellowship. In the latter part of the 19th century, the "Windy City" became a Mecca especially for Danes, Norwegians and Swedes who came to seek their fortunes in the New World.

These early immigrants were mostly young and adventurous folk who had advanced social ideas. One of their first projects was to organize a fraternal society called "Vikingarne" to pay sick benefits and funeral assistance to immigrants. Then they set up a "reading club" for the intellectual advancement of their people so they could get ahead in an English speaking society. In more recent times, they have established scholarships for high school students whose families are members. They also give a full tuition grant for a member to attend the International Summer School at the prestigious Uppsala University in Sweden.

Fiercely proud of their Scandinavian roots, these "Vikings" erected a statue of a prominent Swede, Carl von Linne, which stands in Chicago's Lincoln Park along Lake Michigan. In 1892, the name of the organization was changed to the "Independent Order of Vikings" in order to identify with the culture of their new land.

It wasn't long before new lodges sprung up in the Chicago area where six are active today. Fifty-two local lodges make up the organization in

112

16 states including Colorado, Connecticut, Illinois, Indiana, Iowa, Massachusetts, Michigan, Missouri, Nebraska, New Hampshire, New Jersey, New York, Oregon, Utah, Washington and Wisconsin. Many of the lodges own the buildings where they meet. A newsletter called the "Viking Journal" is published monthly.

The heart of the organization is a life insurance program. This springs from the immigrant days when the Scandinavians needed to look out for each other in a strange world. Junior Clubs for young people under age 16 sponsor sporting events, dinners, parties and instruction sessions to learn Scandinavian dances.

As you would expect, the Independent Order of Vikings is famous for its smorgasbords. Any Scandinavian holiday is an excuse to bring out the food, but especially Christmas, Lucia Day (December 13), Midsummer Day (June 26) and the Oktoberfest.

Every two years a national convention is held. Seventeen officers and members of the Executive Council are elected to govern and promote the organization. I'm indebted to Kristen Johnson of Quincy, Massachusetts, for information on this organization. If you wish to know more about this proud group of Scandinavians, write to their headquarters: Independent Order of Vikings, 200 East Ontario Street, Room 207, Chicago, Illinois 60611. They're people worth knowing.

Independent Order of Vikings logo.

CHAPTER 57

Tracing A
Family Name

I
S IT POSSIBLE TO TRACE a family name to a single point of origin? I'd been curious about the roots of my family name "Fiske," sometimes spelled "Fisk." The name in Norwegian is the infinitive form of the verb meaning "to fish." In America, it occurs only once for every 250,000 family names.

I never had reason to question the Norwegian background of the name, but was curious that it should also be English. When browsing in a public library, I found a reference to a genealogy of Symond Fiske (15th century) published in 1896. It was available from a library in Green Bay, Wisconsin.

Symond Fiske was Lord of the Manor of Stadhaugh, Suffolk County, northeast of London in East Anglia. The English Fiskes in America suspected a Scandinavian origin for the name, but had never identified it.

In the summer of 1976, while attending a seminar at Luther College in Decorah, Iowa, a professor from Norway asked me about my name. I advised him it was Norwegian, but lacked specific information as to the place. To my surprise, he said, "I know exactly where it comes from." This was the beginning of a new adventure for our family.

When visiting Norway in 1977, we were told that every Norwegian Fiske family has its origin on a farm in the Mo parish in Surnadal, about 75 miles southwest of Trondheim. The first time going through Oslo's Gaardermoen Airport, the official checking my passport said, "Going to Trondelag?" He knew.

The English connection, however, was still a mystery until the genealogy of Symond Fiske came to my attention. I showed it to Dordi Glaerum Skuggevik, a jornalist from Norway, who identified the geographical references in England with places in Surnadal. A study of baptismal records and the wills of over 50 Fiske families in Suffolk

County, England, proves that it was a well established name between 1462 and 1635 at Laxfield. "Lax" is the Norwegian word for "salmon." The "Sur" river running through "Surnadal" is one of the most famous salmon streams in Norway and the Fiske farms are located in an area where many salmon are caught. There were other references which also relate Surnadal to Laxfield.

When did they migrate to England? The earliest record of a Fiske in England goes back to 1208, when King John gave land to the men of Laxfield. Among the recipients was a Daniel Fiske. From that time on, the name "John" became a favorite for family use. My journalist friend believes that the migration took place during the Viking days before the Norman conquest of England in 1066. It's my guess that the Fiske families may have emigrated from Surnadal to England shortly after the Battle of Sticklestad, July 29, 1030. It is known that they fought against King Olaf II on the side England's Danish king Knut. Land in England could very well have been their reward.

What about the variation "Fisk?" The record shows that several branches of the family in England dropped the "e." From England, some moved to Ireland and many more to the New England states. One of the earliest in America was Rev. John Fiske who arrived at Cambridge, Massachussets, in 1637. His son, Moses, was the first of many Fiskes to graduate from Harvard College.

When this story first appeared in the Minot Daily News, a copy reached Erwin Fisk of Pasadena, California, editor of the Fisk(e) Family Newsletter. He wrote to me with interest about the Surnadal connection and sent me several copies of the Newsletter. I was interested in discovering that Carlton Fisk, catcher for the Chicago White Sox baseball team, is a member of the English Fisk family.

It interests me that so many bearing the name have had degrees in theology. They seem to have been Evangelicals, many of them Puritans. The number with degrees in law and medicine or who served in the military is also impressive. Those of us who bear this name from the 19th century emigration in Norway are not nearly so numerous as those whose familes came from England. So, if you have a "Fiske" or "Fisk" in your family tree and are English or Irish, it's a good bet that the name traces back to that salmon stream in Surnadal.

CHAPTER 58

Myron Floren
Goes To Norway

THE HEART LONGS TO GO HOME. It was so for Myron Floren, the best known accordionist in America. "Home," in this case was not Webster, SD, where he began life, nor in Rolling Hills, California, where he lives with his family, but Norway, the land of his roots.

Floren has become a favorite with people who attend the Norsk Høstfest in Minot, North Dakota. People return every year from all over the United States and Canada to hear him again. They stand to applaud even before he begins to play the old time polkas, schottishes, waltzes and gospel songs.

The Høstfest sponsored a Norway trip featuring Floren in the summer of 1985. It was conducted by Carrol T. Juven of Fargo, ND, a veteran traveler of more than 50 trips to Norway and whose roots are in Hallingdal. Accompanying the famous accordionist was the "Joe Alme Big Band" ("Stor Band" in Norwegian). Prof. Joseph Alme, Director of the International Music Camp at the Peace Gardens bordering North Dakota and Manitoba, is a popular and respected musician in the Midwest. Many of Floren's friends were along on the tour.

The tour began in Oslo and then travelled over the Haukeli Mountains to Bergen. There they enjoyed a visit with His Honor, Haakon Randal, Governor of Hordaland. They had met two years before at the Høstfest. My wife and I visited Governor Randal a few weeks later in Bergen. He was still excited to have had Floren perform in his capital city.

From Bergen they travelled over the mountain roads and fjords to Skei where they joined in an evening of musical fun with the "Fjellklang Spelemannslag," a group of local entertainers whom Floren had met previously at the Høstfest. From there they travelled across the Geiranger Fjord, down the steep and winding Trollstig Road to Aandalsness. Then they crossed over more mountains and fjords to Trondheim, where Floren traces some of his ancestry. In Trondheim, a women who had seen him perform in America, came on stage during the concert with a big bouquet of roses to present to the famed accordionist, much to the pleasure of the audience.

No trip connected with the Høstfest would be complete without stopping at Skien, Minot's "Sister City." This visit was special because it coincided with the Telemark "Handelstevnet" (Trade Fair). They toured the Porsgrunn Porcelain Factory and visited with its owner, Kjell Strand, who has attended the Høstfest many times.

Floren's popularity in Norway was enhanced by his ability to speak Norwegian. This always surprises our cousins across the sea, especially if we happen to speak with one of the local dialects.

Alme said, "I found our trip to Norway to be both exciting and refreshing." "Exciting" because Floren is an outstanding professional and "refreshing" because of Norway's beautiful scenery and the hospitality its people. Alme, like others on the tour, contacted relatives that they did not know existed. He commented, "travelling and performing with Myron Floren in Norway was one of the greatest experiences one can ever have."

Alme's band members are themselves all outstanding musicians. Every member had to be able to play two or more instruments. Besides Alme from North Dakota, they included Cordell Bugbee, Harlan Helgeson and Robert Quebbemann of Minot; Scott Greenwood of Westhope; Gordon Lindquist of Bottineau; Orville Roble of Harvey; and Guy Shobe of Stanley; Jim Beer and Ed Mantuefel of Winnipeg, Manitoba were also part of the "Big Band."

Receptions were held for Floren and his entourage wherever they visited and press coverage was lavish with praise. The people were captivated with his charming personality and excellent musicianship. They're already waiting for his next "homecoming." Floren hasn't announced when he'll make his next trip to Norway, but he's promised to keep coming back to the Høstfest. They are his most enthusiastic audience anywhere. We hope that will be a long time.

CHAPTER 59

The Tales
Of Askeladden

FOLK TALES TELL A GREAT DEAL about a nation. Every country has its special stories which describe the humor, wit and wisdom by which they have survived. Two Norwegian writers made a great effort to collect the stories of their people before the outside world made its modernizing impact on them. Peter Christian Asbjorsen and Jorgen Moe became friends when they were school boys. They loved to hunt, fish, hike and dream of becoming poets.

Influenced by Grimm's fairy tales from Germany, they travelled up and down the valleys of Norway during the 1840s, especially in Gudbrandsdal and Telemark, listening to the stories which had been told for generations. The people never tired of telling or hearing them again and again. It was their main entertainment during the long dark nights of winter.

Among the favorite stories were those of Askeladden, "the Ash Boy." He was the "Cinderella" of the boy's world. His main job was tending the fire and raking the ashes in the fireplace. His two older brothers scorned him because of his simple honesty. They were "bigshots" in their own eyes. Even his mother merely tolerated him. In the stories Askeladden always comes out on top, much to the chagrin of everyone except the listeners.

Once there was a king whose daughter was an atrocious liar. He offered any man who could get her to say, "You're a liar," that he'd get half the kingdom and the princess for a wife. When the older brothers failed, Askeladden ventured forth to the castle and managed to always tell a taller tale than the princess. He won the prize.

In another story, Askeladden matched wits and courage with a big, burly Troll in the forest. The older brothers had been sent into the forest to chop wood. As soon as the chips started to fly, the Troll would say, "If you're chopping in my forest, I'm going to kill you!" They threw away their axes and ran for dear life until they got home. Askeladden had never been away from home before, but he confidently set out for the forest. When confronted with the Troll, he took some cheese from his knapsack and squeezed it until whey ran out of it and said, "If you don't hold your tongue, I'll squeeze you the way I'm squeezing water out of this white stone." With that, the Troll became cooperative and invited the boy to his home where he challenged him to an eating contest. Fortunately for Askeladden, Trolls are a bit dim witted and have weak eyes. The Ash Boy kept putting the food into his knapsack hanging over his stomach and slit it when full. When the Troll could eat no more, Askeladden advised him to slit his stomach, as he had done to his knapsack. The Troll did so and Askeladden marched home with all the silver and gold found in the mountain.

In another story, the king offered his daughter and half of the kingdom to anyone who could build a ship that could go as fast on land as on sea. The proclamation was read in all the churches of the land. Askeladden had managed to get away from the ashes and be at the service that day. His older brothers set out for the prize and on the way met a bent and wizened old man. When he asked what they were doing, they lied and everything turned out badly.

When Askeladden's turn came, his honesty and wits always carried him through to success, even when the king tried to renig on the deal. He didn't like the Ash Boy's dirty clothes. Finally, he grudgingly gave Askeladden both princess and kingdom.

People never tire of these morality stories where the simple triumph over the wise, the weak over the strong and where honesty pays handsome dividends. The people who lived in the valleys of Norway were mostly poor and these stories kept hope alive even when they had little else than "hope."

CHAPTER 60

The Prime Minister
Who Saved The King

A FTER WORLD WAR II, the Prime Minister of Norway, Carl J. Hambro, was welcomed to America as a hero of the Resistance. When he visited the Buck Ellingson farm near Hillsboro, ND, the newspapers carried front page stories with a picture of him holding one of their children. It was touching. Hambro was regarded as next in importance to the king.

An air raid alarm went off in Oslo at 1:00 a.m. on April 9, 1940. Most people thought it was a routine drill, but Hambro, then President of the Storting (Parliament), immediately checked and found out that foreign men-of-war were steaming up the Oslofjord. He instantly understood the implications and advised King Haakon VII that the Royal Family and Storting members should take the next train to Hamar, 100 miles north. It was imperative that the King and his family should not fall into Nazi hands, as well as the royal gold reserves.

The Storting assembled and passed the necessary emergency legislation for the government to function outside of Oslo. Spies followed their every move. Barely had this been done when enemy war planes began to bomb their locations. They moved 20 miles east to Elverum, where at one point, both the King and Crown Prince Olav took shelter under a large tree during the bombing. If they had been killed, Prince Harald, just three years old, would have had a care-taker appointed for him by the Supreme Court. The Nazis planned to control that appointment and the country would be captive. Deep snow hampered travel through the mountains.

Back in Oslo, Vikdun Quisling, a former army officer, proclaimed himself "Chief of State" and appointed a "government" of virtually unknown people who were horrified when told of their new jobs. Quisling had just returned from seeing Hitler in Berlin two days earlier. Dr. Brauer, the German Minister in Norway, presented a list of demands between 4:30 and 5:00 a.m. which amounted to a complete surrender.

Delaying tactics were used before responding so the Royal Family would have time to travel further away from Oslo. The demands were then rejected.

After two months of heroic defense, the fighting was over in Norway and the government was relocated to London. Crown Prince Martha and her children, Ragnhild, Astrid and Harald, went to the USA where they were the personal guests of President and Mrs. Roosevelt at their Hyde Park home for the duration of the war.

Who was Carl J. Hambro? The Hambros had moved to Norway from England during the Swedish period (1814-1905) and became loyal citizens and significant servants of the nation. But there is an irony in the story. When the famous constitution of May 17 ("Syttende Mai"), 1814, was signed, it excluded Jews from Norway (also Jesuits). Only after this was changed in 1851, was it possible for the Hambros to become "Norwegians." The total number of Jews never exceeded 1500 before the war. But for this reason, Quisling and the Nazis had made a point of attacking Hambro. Throughout the war, he worked tirelessly for Norway's freedom as a leader for the government in exile.

It's a lucky thing that the original constitution was amended, or the Royal Family may have become hostage to Hitler on that fateful morning of April 9, 1940. Norway and Norwegians everywhere contine to honor the name of the Prime Minister who saved the King.

CHAPTER 61

The Anatomy
Of A Story

S EVERAL YEARS AGO when our children were young, I'd tell them stories about Viking tales and exploits. My wife urged me to put the stories into writing so that they could be remembered. One year, when our family was widely scattered, I wrote a weekly newsletter to the children and included a Scandinavian story.

In March 1983, my good friend, Al Larson, bought a newspaper and asked if he could print some of the stories. I agreed, thinking that maybe a dozen or so would be suitable. Now after 300 "Scandinavian Heritage" columns have been published, the stories are still coming every week.

People ask me, "Where do you get your ideas?" Some are personal experiences, some come from my family history or from reading. Some are discoveries made in travelling and others have been told to me by friends. Sometimes new insights come as pieces of information fit together as in a detective story or a jig saw puzzle. How do I decide which to use? If it's interesting to me, then I figure that others might like them too. Almost anything can become a story if the writer's imagination goes to work while doing research.

I do have certain rules for writing. Even though I'm obviously proud of my Norwegian and Scandinavian heritage, I will never "put down" other ethnic groups. There are plenty of reasons for pride in heritage by everyone. In fact, I look for good things to say about others, especially as they relate to Scandinavians.

In the summer of 1982, I was considering a way to share my Scandinavian reading and research. In an almost mystical manner, the idea of a calendar came to mind. The idea was shared with Larson who liked it. He and his business partner at the time, Vance Castleman, published the first "Scandinavian Heritage Calendar." We needed pictures and were fortunate to get acqainted with Buck Jenkins of Bend, Oregon, who furnished them out of his collection of over 10,000 Scandinavian slides. The calendar research became a source for stories.

To my surprise, the public showed a lot of interest in the articles. Letters are occasionally received. Some offered new information. Many stories have been written because people have shared their personal histories with me. People tell me that they clip the stories and put them into scrapbooks or mail them to relatives and friends all over the United States. I've even heard of the articles being sent to South America and to Norway.

One story was about "The Scandinavians in Detroit." Someone in North Dakota sent it to Minnesota. From there it went to Michigan and found its way to Ebba Slomeana, Editor of the "Nordic News," published by the Norse Civic Association in Detroit. She requested permission to reprint it for their Michigan readers. The "Hallingen," a publication of Norwegian-Americans from Hallingdal, Norway, has also reprinted some of the stories. The Columbia Press in Warrenton, Oregon, publishes a Scandinavian newspaper and carries the column, as does the Times of Westby, Wisconsin. When Larson sold his Area Market Review to the Minot Daily News, Terry Greenberg, the Editor, requested that I continue the column. This has been a happy association for me.

Some people like to play golf. Others bowl, play musical instruments or have another outlet for their special energies. I like to write. My first writing job was for the Fargo Forum when I was a high school senior, condensing obituaries from weekly papers. I find writing an enjoyable way to share something of myself with others. Many people asked, "Are you going to put the stories into a book?" Finally, the first volume of 100 stories was published in March 1987. It's about to go into a third printing and now a sequel volume of another 100 stories has been published.

My Danish-American wife, Gerda, has been helpful as a listener and reads the copies before they become final. She's also an avid reader and makes a lot of suggestions for stories. If any of our family are home, they also offer suggestions. Using a word processor for writing makes corrections and revisions easy to do. How long can I keep writing about Scandinavia? For a long time, I hope.

CHAPTER 62

A Visit To
The Bergen Aquarium

W E HUMANS COME IN A variety of sizes, shapes and colors, and think of ourselves as pretty special in God's eyes. But we are alike to the point of being boring in comparison to the almost endless variety of life forms that live in water. I learned a lot about this from my visit to the aquarium in Bergen, Norway.

After 10 years of planning and building, the Bergen Aquarium was opened in 1960. It's located at Nordness Point, formerly a strong fortification, and about a 15 minute walk from the "Bryggen," which used to be the headquarters of the Hanseatic League in western Norway. Nearby, in the midst of the old military installations, is the Institute of Marine Research. It's a 10 story building, containing about 100 offices and laboratories. You can also see a place called "Witches Hill," where Anne Pedersdotter and others were burned at the stake.

Bergen has one of the few aquariums in the world that has unlimited supplies of clean, natural seawater. About 800,000 gallons a day are pumped from about 500 feet deep in the nearby ocean. It's not necessary to filter it as the undercurrent off Nordness Point constantly keeps it renewed. About five miles of pipelines, built of neutral plastic materials, bring both fresh and salt water to the aquarium.

Nine large tanks on the upper floor and 42 smaller displays on the lower floor give an idea of the many kinds of fish which surround Norway's long coast line. The outdoor pool contains seals, porpoises and walruses.

Light, air and water are essential to all life and these are adequately available in this aquarium. When walking through it, you get the feeling of being beneath the surface of the water because the glass in the side walls is at a 135 degree angle. This hides the glass from the viewer.

We first visited the cod family. Mixed in were varieties of catfish.

Diagrams were displayed to show where these fish can be caught along Norway's coastline and how to catch them. I'm amazed at how "scientifically" these creatures are designed. Our modern submarines and aircraft have nothing on the sophisticated equipment built into a codfish. Its pelvic fins are used to find food on the ocean floor. It can detect prey under a flat stone and turn it over. The lateral line on the fish is used to detect noises. It serves as an "early warning system" to tell whether the vibration comes from an oar, the surf or an engine. Sound travels five times as fast under water as in the air. Let fishermen take note!

Other tanks displayed fish that live beneath a wharf, on the sandy bottom or in the deep sea. I never cease to wonder at the anemones, sea urchins, starfish and sea cucumbers. I took special interest in the salmon family and flatfish. One aquarium consists of sharks and rays. There are eight species of sharks in Norwegian waters, some of which are too large for an aquarium. One of the nuisances of the ocean is the Conger Eel because it becomes tangled in fishing nets. Sometimes it's mistaken for a sea serpent. The Crustaceans (lobsters, crabs, crayfish and prawns) have so many thousands of species that no museum can include them all. The prawns begin life as males and become females when fully grown.

How long can a fish live? The halibut can live 60 or more years. Herring may get to be 25 and cod as old as 30. Others may be only two or three years. The age of a fish can be read from its scales, its ear stone or vertebrae. Before fish are put into the aquarium, the air in their swim bladders is removed. They are then re-pressurize in the aquarium.

Fish are as different as people. Some are trusting of their feeders, while others take months to become friendly. There is a lot to learn at an aquarium.

The sea, however, is not as safe as it used to be. Humans have dumped so much petroleum, chemicals, radioactive waste and garbage into it that large areas are no longer safe for life. Maybe the fish in the aquariums are the lucky ones.

CHAPTER 63

Alfred Nobel
And The 'Prizes'

I F YOU TAKE A TOUR of Stockholm, your guide will certainly point out the Grand Hotel and comment, "That's where the Nobel prizes are announced." The awards in physics, chemistry, medicine and literature have been given there since 1901. The award for economics, given only since 1969, is also announced in Stockholm. The politically important Nobel Peace Prize is given out in Oslo.

The man who started the world's most prestigious awards was Alfred Nobel (1833-1896), a Swedish chemist. Nobel's father had been an inventor and made it possible for him to study in St. Petersburg (Leningrad) and in the United States. His international fame came from experimenting with nitroglycerin in his father's factory. In 1867, after years of work, he combined it with an absorbent substance that could be safely shipped. He called it "dynamite," from a Greek work meaning "power." Nobel intended it to be used for peaceful purposes, especially in engineering and in road building.

It wasn't long before Nobel became one of the richest men in the world. He built factories in many countries and purchased the Bofors armament plant in Sweden. Among the other things he experimented on were synthetic rubber and artificial silk. A lover of literature, he wrote several plays and novels. These, however, did not bring him fame.

An idealistic Swede, Nobel's fragile health suffered intense guilt when he saw his prized dynamite being used for war. He had only thought of peace. In his will, an endowment fund of $9,000,000, money from his estate, was set aside for prizes to promote international peace. The value of each prize had reached $180,000 by 1981. The Swedish Central Bank provides the money for the economics prize.

All the awards, except the Peace Prize, are given out in Stockholm. But for some unclear reason, Nobel turned over the management of this award to the Norwegian Parliament (Storting) which appoints a committee of five to make its selection. All the awards are made on

December 10, the anniversary of Nobel's death. Two or more persons may share the prize, or no award may be made at all. No one is allowed to apply for these prizes. Nominations must be made by a "qualified" person.

Immense prestige is connected with the Nobel prizes in addition to the money. I noted this on a trip to Norway in 1985 when I obtained a copy of the Yearbook for the Norwegian (State) Church. The picture of Bishop Desmond Tutu of South Africa was on the front cover. In the American press, hardly a reference is made to the Bishop without noting that he is a "Nobel Peace Prize" winner. The award reflects the feelings of the Norwegian people. They are among the strongest to oppose the Apartheid policies of the South African government. The Scandinavian Air System has stopped flights to South Africa. This recognition of Bishop Tuto has added to his stature as a leader in his country.

To read through the list of awards since they began in 1901 is to review a "who's who" of the world's most influential people in the 20th century. Besides Bishop Tuto, some of the other award winners have been Wilhelm Roentgen, Theodore Roosevelt, Rudyard Kippling, Albert Einstein, Selma Lagerlof, George Bernard Shaw, Niels Bohr, Arthur Compton, Jane Addams, Enrico Fermi, Linus Pauling, Winston Churchill, Dag Hammarskjold, Albert Schweitzer, Milton Friedman, Norman Borlaug, Elli Wiesel and Mother Theresa. Americans have won the largest number of awards, followed by the Germans, English and French. Seven organizations have won awards, including the United Nations High Commission of Refugees. Only two winners have declined to accept, Boris Pasternak (1973) and Jean Paul Sartre (1977), both in literature.

It's a strange twist of events that the Scandinavians, once the terror of western Europe, should now be the world's foremost promoters of peace; and that the invention of dynamite, intended for peace, should now be the stock in trade for terrorists. The $9,000,000 trust fund still speaks eloquently in a time when the money of "influence" is counted rather in the billions.

CHAPTER 64

Impressions of 'Native Americans' By Swedish Immigrants

I GREW UP ON A FARM ten miles west of Ft. Abercrombie, in southeastern North Dakota. During the days of PWA, the fort was restored and there was a big 75th celebration in 1937 to remember the "massacre" of 1862. It was quite a party. Prof. Edward Milligan, Superintendent of Schools in nearby Colfax, led the Indian dances.

By the time I was growing up, our contacts with Native Americans was on a very civil basis. I remember that my father had a hired man one year whose mother was a Sioux. He look every bit a "Native American" and was accepted as one of our family.

Things were not that simple, however, when the first immigrants arrived. Sweden sent more of its people to America than any other Scandinavian country - 1,200,000. Some of the Swedish impressions with the Indians are preserved in letters collected from the immigrant period (1840-1914).

Life in the New World was quite a shock to the highly civilized Swedes. American shysters and swindlers of every sort were set to pounce on unwary immigrants. They had already victimized many of the Native Americans and this caused the immigrants to be in double jeopardy as they travelled across the prairie trails. They also witnessed the savage reprisals against the Indians and the "trail of broken treaties."

Prof. H. Arnold Barton of Southern Illinois University has written that "Though they sometimes feared the red man, there is little evidence that they hated or despised him. On the whole relations were peaceable and the Swedes tended both to respect the Indian and to sympathize with his lot."

One young man, Carl Friman, wrote home to Sweden from Salem, Wisconsin, that the immigrants and the Indians used to hunt deer together. Another immigrant, Peter Cassel, wrote home that the government had purchased land from Indians south of Mt. Pleasant, Iowa, where they intended to establish a Swedish colony. They did and I have driven through this well kept community many times while travelling to St. Louis.

Those about to emigrate from both Sweden and Norway were warned, especially by the clergy, that their trip would be full of dangers. If they did not fall into the hands of Turkish pirates or suffer shipwreck on the way over, the impenetrable forests of America would offer "ferocious wild beasts and bloodthirsty Indians" as their only neighbors.

Other pastors, however, left the security of the state church in Sweden and endured the frontier life. Sometimes they travelled for many days and over many miles of trackless territory to minister to scattered groups of immigrants. One of their anxieties in leaving home was the Indians who sometimes silently entered their houses wanting food. The pastor's wife and children learned how to appear brave. More often than not, all they wanted was food and tobacco, with no intent to do harm.

But people travelling the 1800 miles from Iowa to California for gold encountered thousands of warriors looking for the scalps of lonely travellers. A poisoned arrow found many a mark and harnesses were cut away to steal horses. In 1867, August Andren led a group of Scandinavians into western Nebraska to make railroad ties. At the first suspicious noise around the campfire at night, the order was given to put out the fire as well as their pipes. When no squaws or papooses were with the travelling Indians, the immigrants soon learned to beware. That may be a war party! That same summer, the Indians pulled up the tracks and attacked a train when it derailed. Peter Nyman, writing home from Duluth, MN, told how he was released by his Indian captors after turning over the supply of chewing tobacco he had bought in town for the men in the logging camp. This did not make him a hero back in the camp.

George F. Erickson wrote back to Sweden in 1910 about a story he'd heard in America. A Yankee was boasting to a Swede about the greatness of America. No matter what he claimed, the Swede said, "We have exactly the same thing in Sweden." Finally, the American became angry and said, "I know one thing you don't have in Sweden, you don't have any Indians!" Not to be outdone, the Swede replied, "We have Indians in Sweden too, but we call them Norwegians."

CHAPTER 65

The Historic
Tingvoll Church

"RE MOVE NOT THE ANCIENT landmarks," warned the prophets of Israel. The Tingvoll Church in Nordmore, western Norway, is a classic example of an old site which continues to have meaning in the 20th century.

The Tingvoll Church lies along the route between Molde and Trondheim. We visited there in 1984. A "Ting" or "Thing" was the assembly of free farmers and the "voll" is a grassy meadow. The farmers met there as the local legislative body. Tingvoll was in use for such meetings in the Viking days, even before Christianity came to Norway. It was the custom to build a church on important Viking sites to show the victory of Christ over the Norse gods. If you visit the stave church in Bergen, you'll see a granite cross atop an old Viking mound.

Built in the late 12th century, about 800 years ago, the Tingvoll Church was restored in 1929 by Architect Sivert Glaerum from Surnadal, my ancestral community. Constructed like a fortress, the walls are 40 inches thick and have passages built into them. Churches, like castles, were used both for worship and defense. It is believed that the site has Christian connections since the days of King Olaf Tryggvason who died in 1000.

The furnishings are what especially intrigued me. It contains a Bible from 1589 and candlesticks from 1624. The pews date to 1613. The baptismal font was done by artists from Nuremberg, Germany, and dates somewhere between 1400 and 1600. The chalice is pre-Reformation. The crucifix dates to 1664. On the west wall at the front of the nave is the traditional ship which hangs in Scandiavian churches. This one is a model of a 17th century war frigate, draped with Norwegian flags. Carvings of the four evangelists (Matthew, Mark, Luke and John) are mounted on the pulpit and were believed to have been made by a pupil of El Greco. High above the ornately carved altar are statues of Christ on the cross with his sorrowing mother and a disciple standing beneath.

Noticeable to an American visitor is the absence of windows in these old churches and those that you see are small and high, as you'd expect on a defense installation.

Outside the white stucco covered stone building is the typical country cemetery. On one tombstone from the 1300s is the inscription, "Here lies Ingeborg who married Anders. Pray to God for her soul." On top of the steeple is the weather vane, typical of Norwegian churches.

There is much more to the Tingvoll Church than fancy art work from bygone days. The Nordmore area is famous for its music. It has its own history of folk melodies which have a beauty recognized all over Norway. Edvard Braein (1887-1957), an organist and composer, collected most of the living folk music from the Nordmore area before Norway became bombarded with American and British music. (Now the tendency is to make everyone's music alike by imitating whoever happens to be the current star.) Almost 4000 of his collected melodies were recently discovered in an attic. It has been described as a "cultural bomb in Norway."

An unusual opportunity for people of the Midwest USA was held in the summer of 1986 when three musicians from Nordmore did a Minnesota-North Dakota concert tour. Members of the group included soloist Dordi Bergheim. She requested this tour so she could sing "to her dear relatives in North Dakota." Ola Braein, son of Edvard Braein, is a classical harmonica player. He studied under Sigmund Groven who has performed for the Norsk Høstfest. Tor Strand, one of Norway's young leading organists, is the organist in the Tingvoll Church. Most of the musical arrangements have been done by Henning Sommerro, regarded as one of Norway's leading young composers. This music of Nordmore is to Norway what the Negro spirituals are to America. It's language of the soul.

The mountainous interior of Norway was separated from the European centers of influence so that many of its traditions have continued to this present day. The Tingvoll Church is one of the ancient landmarks of Norway that still stands.

CHAPTER 66

The Scandinavian
Colleges In America

"HOW THEY LOVE EDUCATION. How they will plan and how ready they are to sacrifice and to suffer that their children may have an education. I actually saw large families living in sod shacks on the open prairie sending a boy or a girl to Concordia College." This is how Rev. George H. Gerberding, newly arrived from the East in Fargo, North Dakota, described the Scandinavian passion for education.

The Scandinavian immigration to America happened when an awakening to learning was taking place in their homelands. Norway had recently gotten a university. Bishop Grundtvig was leading a movement in Denmark to make education available for the common people. Finland was just reclaiming its own language for literature and government after hundreds of years of Swedish dominance. Sweden's new ruling family, the Bernadottes from France, embraced the creed of liberty, equality and fraternity.

It was only natural that education was such a high priority in the minds of so many Scandinavian immigrants. The earliest Scandinavian school, named Augustana, began at Chicago in 1860. Being a joint venture of Swedish and Norwegian congregations, it's primary concern was to prepare the sons of immigrants for the ministry. Times were tough. In 1862, the school was lured to Paxton, Illinois, by an offer of the Illinois Central Railroad. In 1869, the Norwegians set up their own school and parted from the Swedes as friends.

From these humble beginnings came Augustana (Swedish) College in Rock Island, Illinois, and Augustana (Norwegian) College in Sioux Falls, South Dakota, and Augsburg College in Minneapolis. "Augsburg," the German name for Augustana (Latin), refers to the "Augsburg Confession" of 1530, a statement of faith accepted by Lutherans. Other Swedish schools include Gustavus Adolphus (1862), St. Peter, Minnesota; Bethany (1881), Lindsboro, Kansas; Upsala (1893), East Orange,

132

New Jersey, and Bethel (Baptist) in St. Paul.

The Norwegians founded Luther College in 1861, when the Union Army closed down Concordia Seminary in St. Louis, because the faculty were said to be sympathetic to slavery. Prior to this, the Norwegian Synod leaders had visited several Lutheran schools and were impressed by the educational system of the Missouri Synod Lutherans. They arranged for some Norwegian faculty to be at Concordia Seminary to tutor the future Norwegian pastors. While the Norwegion faculty in St. Louis favored the arrangement and even defended its views on slavery, the Norwegian congregations would have no part of it. They began a school near LaCrosse, Wisconsin, in a vacant parsonage which moved the following year to Decorah, Iowa.

Later Norwegian schools started in Minnesota were St. Olaf (1874) at Northfield and Concordia (1891) at Moorhead. Pacific Lutheran University (1891) was founded in Tacoma, Washington. Waldorf College (1903) in Forest City, Iowa, Camrose Lutheran College (1911) in Camrose, Alberta, and Luther College (1913) in Regina, Saskatchewan, followed after the turn of the century. There had also been a Clifton College in Clifton, Texas, which was merged with Texas Lutheran at Seguin in 1954. Bethany College, Mankato, Minnesota, was started by Norwegian-Americans in 1926. Norwegians-Americans were also active in starting California Lutheran College at Thousand Oaks near Los Angeles in 1961.

The Danes started two colleges which are still in operation: Dana (1884) in Blair, Nebraska and Grand View (1896) in Des Moines, Iowa. Suomi College in Hancock, Michigan, was begun in 1896 by Finnish immigrants. Besides the above named schools, there were many more smaller colleges and academies (high schools) operated by Scandinavians which have either been merged into larger schools or were closed by the great depression of the 1930s. The only one of those academies operating today in the United States is Oak Grove High School in Fargo, North Dakota, where I received my high school diploma.

What was the driving force behind this passion for education? The Scandinavians were aliens in a strange and not always hospitable land. Establishing schools helped them to retain their ethnic identity and to keep their religious faith as taught in their homelands. It made it possible for many farm youth to get an education with limited ability in English. Since many communities did not have high schools, the academies with a college department provided dormitories and made an education possible for many immigrant children.

Most of the schools started by Scandinavians have chosen not to become universities. There was a movement in the 1950s to make this change. The decision to remain "colleges" prevailed because it was thought better to remain colleges of excellence than to become second class universities. The decision has been vindicated. The Scandinavian-American colleges now serve people of all ethnic backgrounds, but they have not forgotten their heritage.

CHAPTER 67

The Norwegians
Of Lake Wobegon

ARRISON KEILLOR, THE CREATOR of the Lake Wobegon stories is one of America's most interesting folk humorists. His tales about the mythological Minnesota village told on American Public Radio's "Prairie Home Companion" had listeners all over the United States. His book, "Lake Wobegon Days," (1985) soared immediately to the top of the best seller lists and was featured as a Book of the Month Club selection.

Two ethnic and religious groups are in the center stage of Lake Wobegon. They are the German Catholics and the Norwegian Lutherans. Keillor himself was brought up in the Plymouth Brethren denomination, a small group of English evangelicals. He shows himself an astute sociologist who can put every object and event into the position of humor.

I'm fascinated how he came to know his neighbors so well. The very sensitive person, I suppose, may take offense at his observations. But most people are likely to enjoy the laughs, especially those on their own group. You get the feeling that he's got some strong admiration for both his German and Norwegian neighbors. A new ethnic group, the Danes, came into the script after his marriage in Copenhagen.

The two visible organizations in town are the Knights of Columbus with their impressive uniforms and showy parades, and the Sons of Knute who trudge along with gusto, when occasion requires.

Among the noted Norwegians in town is the Ingqvist family. They own the bank and occupy the pulpit of Lake Wobegon Lutheran Church. The Norwegian car dealership, owned by the Bunsens, sells Fords. It's a matter of "faith" to buy the right car as the Catholics drive Chevies sold by the German Kreugers. He notes that the Plymouth Brethren also drive Fords (why not Plymouths?), but have a Bible verse on a small steel plate bolted on top of the licenses. The Norwegian banker, however, drives a Lincoln.

Keillor is pretty good in picking up on lutefisk and all such things as distinguish Norwegians from other people. He makes the same mistake as most Norwegians, however, in designating May 17, 1814 ("syttende Mai") as "Independence Day" when it's really "Constitution Day." It took another 91 years (1905) until Norway was fully free and elected a king of its own choice. You can't blame Keillor for that. He only tells it like he hears it.

Some of the other Norwegians memorialized in the Lake Wobegon stories are Senator Thorvaldson, and the Anderson, Berge, Fjelde, Johnson, Oleson, Qvist, Tollefson and Tollerud families. The Norwegians were able to change the name of the town in 1880 from New Albion to Lake Wobegone when they gained a 4-3 majority on the City Council. After quite a squabble, it finally got changed to "Wobegon." The Lake Wobegon Norwegians came from Stavanger, Telemark and Hallingdal. They were attracted to Lake Wobegon by the rocky soil. It was just like home.

Keillor has his information pretty straight on how Norwegians think Christmas should be celebrated. Some things can only learned from "being there." He knows that every Norwegian must sing "Jeg er saa glad hver Julekveld" ("I am so glad each Christmas Eve") at least 12 times during the holidays or it just won't be Christmas. And it always brings tear-filled eyes to the Sons of Knute. "Julekake" (Christmas bread) is also essential for a real Christmas. Lutefisk, however, is a more serious matter. It's not for everybody. Not even all Norwegians have sturdy enough stomachs and nostrils to indulge. That's probably why the Vikings were so tough, since the ordeal for becoming a true Viking was to eat six consecutive meals of lutefisk. The Viking chiefs didn't want to take any sissies along on their raids of England, Ireland and France.

There is more than a little truth when Keillor describes the true Norwegians as being suspicious of pleasure. It always seems to produce a bad conscience. He footnotes them as saying, "If you broke your leg, walk home and apply ice. Don't complain. Don't baby yourself." It's really not that tough today, but I've known some for whom it applied. He has also learned the commonly used Norwegian words and expressions well.

Lake Wobegon has one unique attraction, the "Statue of the Unknown Norwegian." It was made by an Irishman in 1896. (If he could have spoken Norwegian, he might have found out the man's name!) After being damaged in a storm in 1947, it was moved into the local museum alongside the Lake Wobegon runestone which "proves that Viking explorers were here in 1381." On Columbus Day, the runestone is carried to the school so the children can learn who really discovered America. It's gospel for them that this land should be called "The United States of Erica," instead of "America." Afterall, it was Erik the Red's son, Leif, who actually set foot on this continent 500 years before that Italian mapmaker (Amerigo Vespucci) ever heard about the place. If you happen to visit Lake Wobegon, be sure to sign the visitor's book supplied by the Sons of Knute.

Garrison Keillor's contribution to Americana may have started something that is just as true as motherhood and good as apple pie. But alas! Keillor's departure from our favorite Saturday program has brought a pall of sorrow over those who waited patiently each week for the news from Lake Wobegon. We're concerned about those good people and Keillor is our only contact. His move to Copenhagen was understandable so his wife could enjoy "wonderful Copenagen." But now he lives in the "Big Apple." Does New York City appreciate him? Time may have forgotten that town in Minnesota, but we haven't. There are lot's of us shy people waiting to hear the latest news about the Tolleruds, the Sons of Knute and their neighbors. Come back, Mr. Keillor. We haven't been the same since you left us.

CHAPTER 68

Johan Falkberget —
Novelist From The Copper Mines

JOHAN FALKBERGET AND THE CITY of Røros in Norway may be two of the best kept Scandinavian secrets. Røros is located on the eastern route between Trondheim and Oslo. UNESCO's World Heritage List includes Røros together with the pyramids of Egypt and the redwood forests of California as tourist attractions. It was founded in 1644 by Lorentz Lossius, a German business man, who was given permission to develop the newly discovered copper mines. The area had been virtually uninhabited since the Black Death days (1349) when two out of every three Norwegians died.

It was not unusual that German miners were invited into Norway by the Danish king, Christian IV. Norwegians were poor and inexperienced in mining. Germans, however, had been operating mines for centuries and many of them had the money required to get the work started. As a result, Røros is a community of people with Germans, Norwegians and Swedes today. This gives it a distinct racial mix.

Johan Falkberget (1879-1967) lived most of his life in the Røros community and it provided him with the setting for the majority of his novels. In his writings, Røros is known as "Bergstaden" ("mining town"). Its high altitude, sharp contrasts in climate, closeness to the Swedish border and its great church towering over the wooden cottages give it the background for fascinating stories. Falkberget's father was a mine foreman who also farmed in his spare time. Schooling was limited to a boy in such a situation as he was needed at home for work. The future novelist began working at the mines when he was eight. But he persisted and got whatever education he could. At age 14, he was writing articles for the local newspaper. He left the mines when 27 and became editor of a newspaper in Alesund, but soon moved to Oslo.

His writings showed a deep social conscience which revolted against the oppression of the privileged classes over the working people. In 1922, at age 43, he returned to Røros to take over the family farm which he inherited. This provided the setting for his writing the history of his home community. "The Fourth Night Watch" ("Den fjerde Nattevakt," 1923) began his most famous series of novels.

The setting of this story is early nineteenth century and the principle character is Benjamin Sigismund (based on an actual person), the newly arrived pastor from Copenhagen. He was a handsome man with all the qualities of charm, except patience, which he eventually learned from an alcoholic klokker (deacon), who was the local blacksmith. His wife, Kathryn, was a sickly person who had difficulty enduring the rugged Røros climate. She would have liked her husband to become a bishop so they could move to a better place. Much to his own surprise, Sigismund became firmly attached to this place of harsh life and customs.

Before 1813, all Norwegian clergy were educated in Denmark because Norway didn't have a university. Copenhagen, being a city of culture, retained a strong nostalgia, especially for many first ladies of the parsonage. They felt a superior position over the "natives" who had not travelled beyond their valleys.

Just before leaving Copenhagen, a gypsy woman warned Sigismund against having anything to do with a woman dressed in red that he'd meet in the churchyard early one morning. His first reaction was to discount as fiction what a dirty old hag told him. Afterall, he was an educated man with a university degree and would certainly not compromise his professional ethics. Fatefully it happened early one morning, while answering a pastoral request for help, the young woman in red passed him. He momentarily became white with fear.

The woman, Gunhild, was the neice of the klokker and about to be married to a man she loathed. But since he had a good job and money, her mother pressured her to accept the offer. The old uncle got the pastor's ear about her dilemma. This set the trap to fulfill the gypsy woman's prophecy.

Sigismund was not a willing victim of temptation. He had, however, a rigid streak of predestination and fate, and had a big heart which responded to every need for pastoral care, no matter how difficult. He once braved the fiercest blizzard to minister to a Lapp family. Gunhild's wedding was performed and this began the spinning of the web that was to finally enmesh his conscience and reputation.

Following a series of tragedies in which Gunhild's husband committed suicide and his own wife died, Sigismund's health broke and he came down with consumption. He conducted his last service while hardly able to stand erect. He put forth a powerful effort and entranced the congregation which suddenly saw him to be a prophet of God whom they had not understood or appreciated. The old blacksmith had been his only loyal friend through his time of depression. In the final pages, both pastor and klokker died, and Gunhild remained to mourn them both.

Falkberget was a powerful writer and deserves more American readers. Even if you have not been to Norway, you will be quickly drawn into his stories and will lay the book down reluctantly only because you are finished. His writings hold an additional fascination for me since my second cousin, Kaare Rogstad of Orkdal, was once the pastor of the Røros church which King Olav V honored with his presence on its 200th anniversary.

CHAPTER 69

Scandinavian Immigrant
Worship Traditions

IMMIGRANTS LEAVING SCANDINAVIA for the New World received little sympathy and support from the established churches of their lands. They did not, however, abandon their faith and religious upbringing. Most of them remembered their instruction in Bible and catechism. They held a veneration for the church building, respect for an educated and ordained clergy and a sense of order and beauty in worship.

Since 98% of the people from Scandinavian countries regarded themselves as members of the Evangelical Lutheran Church, the majority became attached to new Lutheran congregations on the American frontier. There were, however, some who had joined non-Lutheran congregations while still in Europe, namely Methodists, Baptists and Swedish Covenant. The Scandinavians were unprepared for the religious diversity of the American frontier. Many joined whatever denomination happened to be handy and often lost contact with their Scandinavian heritage.

The Norwegians were the most successful in retaining immigrants for their heritage in America. One reason is that they were divided into several Lutheran denominations and often isolated from other people. Large numbers of Swedes became a part of the Augustana Synod. Danes were the most likely to become a part of the American "melting pot." The Finns and Icelandic people also established their own denominations. Ever since 1890, merger movements have been prominent among Scandinavian Lutherans and in 1988 it became virtually complete in the newly formed "Evangelical Lutheran Church in America."

There were two basic centers of influence for worship among Scandinavian immigrants. Danish language and customs helped shape worship in Norway and Iceland. Swedish influence has been strong in Finland.

Worship among Danes has been enriched by three great hymn

141

writers: Hans Brorson, Thomas Kingo and N. F. S. Grundtvig. More than 500 of their hymns are still found in the current Danish hymnal, even though only 15 are used in the Lutheran Book of Worship used in America. Religion among the Danes has always, even from pre-Christian times, combined personal faith and community life. This especially came to the fore in the work of Bishop Grundtvig (1783-1872). Danes like to keep their liturgies simple, with scripture, sermon and sacrament central.

Both Danes and Norwegians employed a "Klokker." This was a layman (deacon) who opened and closed the service with a prescribed prayer. No layman would presume to usurp the role of the pastor, but there was a definite place for him in worship. In America, Norwegians were the most divided between those who favored the "high mass" of Norway or a simpler order of worship. In almost all cases, the pastor was president of the congregation. This did not change until the 1950s in most rural congregations. In 1952 when I became pastor of the Mylo, Ox Creek and Wolford Lutheran congregations in north central North Dakota, I was also president of the congregations according to their constitutions. I arranged for the election of a lay vice president who presided at annual meetings until the constitutions could be changed.

The Swedes had the most elaborate liturgy. Like the Norwegians, the Swedes liked a chanted service. This was reassuring to the immigrants when they heard their services in the New World intoned with the familiar sounds of home. Then they felt that God was with them. The Finns also preferred the chanted liturgy.

The most familiar symbol of the Scandinavian clergy was the "Prestkrag," a ruffled collar worn by the clergy in pioneer days. Andreas Ueland, in his book "Recollections of An Immigrant," calls it a "Henry-The-Eighth collar." It's still used in Scandinavia today. On my last trip to Norway, I wanted to buy one and found out that it had to be ordered from Denmark. Fortunately, a cousin in the ministry had an extra one and gave it to me. The black gown ("Prestrock") was a sign of pastoral authority from God. Bishop Bo Giertz of Gothenburg, Sweden, described in his book, "The Hammer of God," the importance of this garment to the pastor's own sense of the ministerial office. Purple was often the only liturgical color used on the altar and pulpit. The Church Year

142

was faithfully followed.

Holy communion was the most serious experience of worship. Four times a year (or less) was considered "safe." Scandinavians took repentance seriously as preparation for the sacrament. They were conditioned to be introspective about sin. However frightening, holy communion had a profound effect for spiritual healing among them. In Rolvaag's "Giants in the Earth," Beret found sanity through the sacrament. Swedish Lutherans practiced fasting before communion.

Scandinavian Lutherans have emphasized congregational freedom and authority, in contrast to their German Lutheran cousins who have put more power into the hands of the bishops, pastors and councils. The concern for local authority goes back to the "Thing" assemblies of free farmers in Viking days. It's a strange fact that Scandinavia had the freest society in the ancient world. Even kings needed their approval to rule.

The immigrant church among Scandinavians was a man's domain. The role of women was to rear children, operate the Ladies Aid, teach Sunday School and keep the home. This might include milking the cows and slopping the hogs. But voting, preaching and governing was the exclusive right of men. They also sat on different sides of the aisle. These "cultural" characteristics of the faith have largely changed in our time, but the passion for "freedom" and the need to be "serious" still dominates Scandinavian worship life in America.

Typical Scandinavian Immigrant Church.

CHAPTER 70

The Fritjof
Saga

HIGH ON THE MOUNTAIN overlooking the fjord across from Balestrand in western Norway, stands the statue of Fritjof. Not far away on the same height is the statue of King Bele, after whom the beach (strand) is named. They are looking in opposite directions.

The statues were a gift from Kaiser Wilhelm II of Germany who used to vacation each summer through 1913 at the Kvikne Hotel in Norway's "westlands." This was his way of showing appreciation for the month each summer that he'd spend in this place of unusual beauty.

Fritjof was the son of Torstein, a real Viking who lived on the farm called Framnes (now Vangsness). Interestingly, this was the birthplace of Frederick of Vangsness, great grandfather of Walter Mondale, former Vice President of the the United States. Time magazine carried a story in 1984 which stated that if Frederick had not moved to his wife's farm (Mundal) and taken her name when he got married, that the former presidential candidate would have been known as Fritz Vangsness. Fritz (or, Frederick) is another name for Fritjof.

King Bele and Torstein had been good friends. They lived in the seventh century, 400 years before St. Olaf (d. 1030). He was considered a good king. He warned his sons, Helge and Halfdan, to keep friendship with Fritjof, for the son of Torstein was a mighty warrior.

The King had an attractive daughter, Ingeborg the "fair," the most beautiful girl in the kingdom, known for her golden hair. (At that time, Norway was divided into many small kingdoms.) And since they were both well born, they lived for a time in a foster home where they were educated for their futures. Fritjof and Ingeborg became fast friends. And when the time for romance came into their hearts, they felt for each other. But by this time old King Bele had died and so had Torstein.

Ingeborg's brothers served jointly as kings and refused the warrior's request to wed their sister, saying "Our sister was not for a vassal born. A King's son alone shall Valhalla's beautiful daughter own, but our serf you may be." Despite his wooing and offer to prove his worthiness with the sword, the local assembly ("Thing") agreed that Fritjof should be banished to the Orkney Islands for a year. If he returned with the taxes which the Jarl owed the Vangsness kings, he should have his bride.

Fritjof returned within the year with the tribute from the Orkneys. But alas, it was too late. Another King, Ring from the Eastland, now claimed the hand of Ingeborg. Ring was an older man and mighty in war. When the brothers refused to accept his offer, Ring brought his army to bring her to his farm by force and to the altar of Balder for the marriage rite. (Balder was one of the gods in the Norse pantheon together with Odin, Thor, Frey and others.) Fritjof accepted his fate as the anger of the gods, though he knew himself to be a worthy man and that King Bele had wished him to be his son-in-law. In anger, Fritjof burned Balder's temple.

Then he took to sea in a magic boat named Ellida, which could speak to him. For several years he rode the waves until he could stand it no longer. He returned to King Ring's banquet hall at Juletide, not to claim a bride but to see her just once more. He entered disguised as a "greybeard," wearing a wild bear's skin. But when insulted by a guard, with feat of strength he lifted him high and turned him upside down.

This got the King's attention and he demanded to know who this stranger might be. When he removed his garb, the King and all could see it was Fritjof, the mighty warrior. The Queen's cheeks paled. King Ring, gracious in manner, invited the warrior to spend a year. In the spring, when the hunts began, the King became exhausted and rested with Fritjof as his guard. Fritjof fought the temptation to behead his rival and claim the Queen. Being found faithful, the King made him his "son," and said "Thou seest I am aged grown, and to the grave must soon recline. Then take thou to my realm, and take the Queen for she is thine."

It happened soon afterwards that the old King gathered his friends and in true Viking fashion committed suicide so that he would go directly to Valhalla (the Viking "heaven"). The people quickly elected Fritjof to wear the crown and wed the Queen. He agreed to be their king, but much to their surprise refused the Queen, saying he would choose his own bride. This was his way of not becoming beholden to them.

While visiting his father's grave to seek wisdom, he was guided by a vision to rebuild the temple of Balder. Soon afterwards, he was reconciled to the sons of King Bele and took Ingeborg to wed. "Ingeborg over Balder's altar gave her hand to him her childhood's friend and her heart's delight." It ended as a hero's story ought. Fritjof won his prize, but only after years of toil and proving himself a worthy man.

There's a lesson in the story. Whatever the prize you seek, first prove your worthiness to possess it. Fritjof still stands guard over the fjord at Vangsness across from Balestrand. The only way to get there is by ferry. I hope you can visit Balestrand some day and wish for you a day of sunshine as it was for us. Take a look at the top of the hill where the Kaiser's gifts still stand. It has become a part of the Scandinavian heritage.

CHAPTER **71**

Lady Inger
Of Austraat

C AN THE INFLUENCE of one person shape a nation and the
future generations of its people? Could a woman have such
power? Since most historians have been men, it should not
surprise us that some outstanding women have gone unnoticed.

Such is the case with Lady Inger of Austraat, who lived north of
Trondheim in Norway. She even escaped the attention of the famed Yale
historian, Roland Bainton, when writing a three volume work on
"Women of the Reformation." I'm indebted for much of my information on her to Prof. Kenneth Christopherson of Pacific Lutheran University in Tacoma, Washington.

Born about 1475 of a long line of Norwegian nobility, Inger inherited
great wealth in money, property and land. Married at age 19 to a
famous knight, Nils Henrikson, she became the mother of five
daughters, three of whom married Danish noblemen. But it was not until her husband's death, when she was 48, that her genius for power was
recognized.

Many, if not most, great events of history cannot be predicted. It often
happens that seemingly unimportant circumstances become major hap-
penings. It was such a meeting of occurrences that took place in the 16th
century as the Reformation spread from Germany to Norway.

It started in Denmark during the power struggle between King
Frederik I, a Lutheran sympathizer, who was struggling to establish his
rule, and the deposed king, Christian II, whose fortunes were tied to
the papal power in Rome.

Vincens Lunge, a prominent Danish nobleman with three doctorates
(philosophy, Roman law and canon law), went to Norway in 1523 on
an errand for Frederik I. While there, he married Inger's daughter. Shortly afterwards, Inger's husband died and the young nobleman took over

the management of her estates and remained permanently in Norway.

Lunge's brilliant mind understood the use of power and soon convinced western and northern Norway to recognize Frederik's claim to rule. It wasn't long before large additional areas of land fell under Inger's control. Some of these lands were confiscated from the church, which was the largest landowner in Norway. This brought Inger into conflict with Archbiship Olaf Engelbriktson of Trondheim. When necessary, the Archbishop also raised armies to enforce the church's claims. Soon there was open war between them for reasons of real estate and religion. Lunge was also rewarded by King Frederik for his loyalty by giving him a monastery in Bergen and its 272 outlying farms. This is not the first time that nobility, kings and bishops had been in conflict. In these struggles, the masses of people were usually ignored, but they paid for the conflicts with their property and blood.

Christian II, the Danish king in exile, landed an army in Oslo to lay seige to Akerhus Castle and regain his kingdom. Another of Inger's sons-in-law, Nils Lykke, was sent by Frederik with a fleet to rescue the city. Christian again went into exile, but finally surrendered at Oslo and was imprisoned by Frederick I in Denmark and spent the rest of his life in a Danish prison.

The struggle between the Archbishop and Lady Inger was ultimately a disaster for both of them. There were instances where they joined forces, but not for long. Lunge and Lykke died treacherously at the Archbishop's direction. When the new Danish king, Christian III, declared "Lutheranism" to be the official church of Denmark and Norway in 1536, Engelbriktson fled Norway. As he left, he plundered Inger's home at Austraat of much of its treasures.

Inger obtained new Danish husbands for her bereaved daughters, but of lower status in nobility. In 1555, at the age of 80, she suffered shipwreck on a trip to Bergen and was drowned. She has been called "the last representative of Norway's old nobility" and combined an unusual mixture of talent, ambition and thirst for power.

All the contestants in this power struggle were jealous for Norwegian independence and were sincere in what they believed was right both towards God and country. But the tide of events was on the side of

Inger and her Danish sons-in-law.

Ever since Emperor Contantine the Great (305-337) decided to combine the Roman Empire with the kingdom of God, the church has had the "protection" of the Caesar's sword. It has also paid the price of becoming the "pawn" of the world's great power brokers. Just as the original conversion of Norway to Christianity was accompanied by violence, so also was its Reformation.

Lady Inger played no small part in these events which have had such a major influence on latter-day Norwegians. One of the mysteries of the human story is that despite the exploitations of Jesus' gospel, both by friends and foes, its influence continues to keep faith and love alive in the most difficult times.

CHAPTER 72

Erik
The Red

ANCIENT ICELAND LACKED the natural resources to build a society of culture. It had no forests, no metals and was not known for music. But Iceland excelled in literature and law. Its creativity was expressed in words. The long dark winters gave plenty time to write. The need to kill off most of their cattle provided adequate calf skins for vellum on which to record their stories. The coming of Christianity in 1000 gave them the Latin alphabet and a writing style.

It's fortunate that Icelandic people have had such literary production. Without their gift to the world, we might not have known about one of the most exciting chapters in human history, the story of Erik the Red and the Norsemen's discovery of America.

Erik was born in Norway. While yet an infant, his father, Thorvald, was exiled for murder and set sail for Iceland. When Erik grew up, he also got into a brawl and with his sword revenged the killing of two of his slaves (probably Irish). Iceland, being a land of law and order, banned him for three years.

To save his life, Erik sailed off into the unknown seas to the west until he came to a vast ice cap (715,000 square miles) which turned out to be Greenland. He explored until he found some grassy areas on the southwest coast. When the three years of exile were up, Erik returned to Iceland, a hero for his discovery. He told them that this new land to the west should be called "Greenland," knowing it to be a lie. But the sagas quoted him as saying, "Men will be more readily persuaded to go there if the land has an attractive name." He became a success in real estate!

After one winter in Iceland, Erik gathered 25 ships, crowded with 1000 people and domestic animals, and sailed to Greenland. Fourteen ships survived the journey. It was 995, the year that Olaf Tryggvason became king of Norway.

That same year, a young sailor named Bjarni travelled from Norway to Iceland with a ship full of goods for trading. Upon arrival, he learned that his father, Herjulf, had left for Greenland with Erik. Determined to see his father, he sailed westward in search of the new land. Everything went wrong. Calm and fog set in. Then the north winds blew. When land appeared, it was not Greenland but the coast of North America, perhaps Cape Cod.

Bjarni did not allow the crew to go ashore, but kept on sailing past what may have been Nova Scotia and Newfoundland. Finally, he reached Greenland and was reunited with his father. They lived there for many years.

Erik was proud of his red hair and beard. It was the same color as Thor's, his hero-god. He also shared his pagan god's values. His three sons, Leif, Thorstein and Thorvald held a lot of promise. His one daughter, Freydis, was illegitimate. Leif was the most adventuresome of the sons and sailed off to Norway. While there, he fell under the spell (and the power) of King Olaf Tryggvason in Trondheim, who had him instructed in the Christian faith and baptized. Leif really didn't have much choice. Olaf was a determined evangelist. But it was an opportunity for him to get ahead.

When it was time to return to his family, the king said, "You are to go to Greenland on a mission for me, to preach Christianity there." Leif was more than a little alarmed to face his Thor-worshipping father with such news. He told the king that it would be a hard task. But the king replied that he had not seen a man better fitted for the job, saying, "You will bring it good luck!" That's how he got the name "Leif the Lucky." The king also held several hostages and sent "protection" to insure the success of the mission.

Leif's mother, Thjodhild, became a quick convert and had a church built near her house, under the rule of a priest sent by the king. His brothers also accepted the new faith, but Erik remained a staunch pagan. To him, the new religion threatened the very foundation of Viking society. Thjodhild, his wife, refused to live with him again. That was his penalty for "unbelief." It may also have been her revenge for Erik's illegitimate daughter.

Leif was burning with curiosity about the new land which had been

sighted by Bjarni Hjerulfson. He bought Bjarni's large ship and assembled a crew of 35. Leif begged his father to lead the expedition. Erik,
however, pleaded that he was too old, but was finally persuaded. On
the way to the ship, his horse stumbled and Erik fell off, claiming that
his foot was injured. Turning to Leif, he said: "You, my son, and I may
no longer travel together." He was talking both about voyages and
religion. Erik remained a loyal pagan to the end. This meant he couldn't
be buried with his family in the consecrated ground of the church
cemetery.

Erik had some admirable qualities and some not so good. But there
is no doubt that he was a brave man and a good colonizer. The communities he established lasted about 400 years. Then they disappeared
during the "Little Ice Age" of the 15th century. But without his courage
and adventurous spirit, "Vinland" may never have been discovered and
Columbus may not have taken his journey westward in 1492. It's recorded that Columbus spent time in Iceland gathering information about
Vinland before sailing off to the "New World" which has become a home
for so many of us.

CHAPTER 73

Where Is
'Vinland?'

FOR MANY YEARS, people were skeptical about the Leif Erikson story of discovering America. In recent years, new evidence has come to light which leaves little doubt that Norsemen not only arrived in America, but had settlements in what they called "Vinland the Good."

People, however, are still curious about Vinland's location. Do we have any idea where the Norse explorers touched the North American continent? Frederick J. Pohl has written an intriguing book entitled "The Viking Settlements of North America." The title may be misleading since these Norsemen were "Christian colonists" rather than "pirates," as the name "Viking" suggests. But it is an exciting commentary on the saga of Erik the Red written by Icelandic scholars in the Middle Ages. Pohl claims that this saga is highly reliable. It has 60 hand drawn maps to show Norse locations.

Most of the proposed sites for the Norse settlements in North America suggest the Maritime Provinces of Canada. Pohl, however, claims that they followed 3000 miles of coastline down to Florida.

The first Norseman to see the New World was Bjarni Herjulfsson who discovered it by accident when sailing from Iceland to Greenland. Leif the Lucky, son of Erik the Red, picked up on his story and spent a winter somewheres in the new land. He made three landings with a crew of 35.

Departing from Brattahlid in the Eastern Settlement of Greenland (actually the southwest tip of the island), Leif sailed past Helluland ("Flat Rock Land") and Markland ("Forestland") until coming to Vinland, which Pohl identifies with Cape Cod. There he built a campsite near a plentiful source of good drinking water, timber and defensive positions, in case there should be hostile natives. It was called "Leif's Shelters" and was 18 feet wide and 52 feet long, large enough to house 36 men. It had sod walls, like houses in Greenland. Nearby was a shelter for his ship.

The name of Leif's place has come to be called "Vinland" because there were many grapes there. One of his sailors was from Germany and knew how to make wine. No doubt, this made the winter seem shorter. The next summer, Leif returned to Greenland. He never made a second trip to the New World since his father died (possibly from pneumonia) and the leadership of Greenland fell to him.

The task of further exploration was picked up Leif's brother Thorvald. He took a crew of 30 men and found "Leif's Shelters." Their first job was to gather up food and fuel for the winter. In the spring of 1007, they began the coastal exploration which required two seasons. Leaving the majority of his men behind to plant crops and cut timber, Thorvald started to explore the new land. An accident broke the keel of the boat and they were stranded until they could cut a new one from the forest.

Then came an historic meeting. The Norsemen encoutered "Native Americans" whom they called "Skraelings," meaning "Shriekers" or "War Whoopers." It was the first time that Europeans coming from the east met Asiatics coming from the west. It was also a tragedy. Finding nine natives aleep under their boats, they captured eight. Prisoners, however, can be inconvenient, so they killed them. But one escaped and returned with a war party. Thorvald did not seem to have thought about retaliation and took a nap. Getting to their ships in the nick of time, they ably defended themselves except for Thorvald who died from an arrow wound. He was the first European to be buried in America, with a cross planted at both his head and feet.

A year later, the Norsemen returned to Greenland. It had been Leif's intention to establish a Christian colony in Vinland. The family's immediate concern was to bring back Thorvald's body so it could be buried in consecrated ground, since it was impractical for a priest to travel to Cape Cod. This task fell to the other brother, Thorstein. His journey was also tragic. Becoming lost at sea, he became ill and died the following year in Greenland.

This did not end the Norse journeys to the New World, though only a few of these explorations have been recorded. In addition to the sagas, letters sent to the Vatican confirm this evidence. Bishop Gnupsson of Greenland visited Vinland in 1117. Otto of Bremen, a well known historian, wrote in 1076 about "Wineland," based on information he had received from the Danes.

In addition to Pohl, Gwyn Jones, a noted Celtic scholar from the University of Cardiff in Wales, has written "The Norse Atlantic Saga." He contends for a smaller area of Norse exploration. James Robert Enterline's "Viking America: The Norse Crossings and Their Legacy" has an epilogue by Thor Heyerdahl which attests to extensive knowledge of the New World in 11th and 12th century Europe. Recently Heyerdahl has been researching this information in the Vatican Library. We await his findings.

The most publicized place for Norsemen in America is L'Anse au Meadows in Newfoundland which the Canadian government has set aside as a national historical site. It was likely occupied for just a short time, but archaeological evidence points to a Norse settlement. It probably should not be identified with Leif Erikson's "Vinland," the location of which may never be known. That there was such a place, however, should not be doubted. Back in Europe, all of the New World was called "Vinland."

Vinland grapes.

CHAPTER 74

The Tale Of
Thorfinn Kalrsefni

WHEN LEIF ERIKSON COULD not make a second voyage to Vinland, the leadership for the explorations fell to Thorfinn Karlsefni. One of the most distinguished of the great Norsemen, he had descended from an illustrious line of Danish, Swedish, Norwegian, Irish and Scottish ancestors. A cousin of Leif, they were both distant cousins to George Washington. He belonged to a select group that they called "Great Vikings," since he was the master of a ship which had crossed the ocean and had become wealthy from his trading voyages.

A hundred years earlier, these Norsemen would have obtained their wealth by raiding monasteries and churches, but since the coming of Christianity to Norway, Iceland and Greenland, they now became rich through trading. They used to endure by "Thor's luck," now they sailed with "Christ's help."

Some historians claim that Thorfinn Karlsefni was the greatest of all the Norsemen, even greater than Leif Erikson. His accomplishments would not dispute this claim. Leif lent him his buildings in Vinland and he set sail with men, women, cattle, sheep and pigs. It should be noted that a thousand years ago, these animals were only about half the size and a quarter of the weight of those today. Selective breeding has greatly increased their size.

When they arived at Leif's Shelters, it wasn't long before the "Skraelings" (Native Americans) came to trade with them. Just as the bargaining was going good, Thorfinn's bull came charging out of the trees, bellowing loudly. The visitors fled with their bundles of fur and other skin wares, but returned in a short time again for business. The one thing that Karlsefni would not trade to them was weapons. They treated the Indians to a taste of milk and they were so utterly taken by it that they gladly gave up all their valuable furs for another taste. After this episode, the Norsemen built a strong fence around the encampment and a palisade around the main house.

Thorfinn's wife, Gudrid, an unusually beautiful and talented woman, gave birth to the first European child born in the New World. They named him Snorri. When I first read about this in the sagas, it hit me like a thunderbolt. I was reared on a farm in southeastern North Dakota and had been active in 4-H and farming. Among the County Agents in our area were two brothers of Icelandic descent named Thorfinsson, one of whom was named Snorri, after the first European born in this land. I'm still impressed with the connection.

It was inevitable that an armed clash would come between the Norsemen and the Skraelings. It happened one day when one of the Skraelings tried to steal some weapons and was killed. Knowing their fear of his bull, Karlsefni used the animal to charge into the enemy camp. It produced the desired effect.

Exploration of the new land was the Norsemen's chief interest. They spent four winters in Vinland, with part of the group tending Leif's Shelters, and the rest searching the coastlands. They were careful never to allow those who went on ahead to get too far away. King Olaf Tryggvason had given Leif two Irish slaves that were swift runners. They were loaned to Thorfinn for exploration. After scouting 48 hours, they'd return with grapes, wheat and other discoveries. One expedition, led by Thorhall (a Thor worshipper), became lost and landed on the west coast of Ireland where they were enslaved and killed.

Frederick J. Pohl has identified the New York harbor as one of Thorfinn's points of exploration. He traces their journey past the coasts of New Jersey, Delaware, Maryland and Virginia where they looked in on every bay and river. One of these, Pohl claims, was the James River, the site of an English colony 600 years later. Journeying southwards, they encountered more natives, some friendly, others not. Where possible, they traded. Once again, Thorfinn's bull ruined the party as he charged out of the woods and the Skraelings fled. This time they returned with a secret weapon of terror. They put a hornet's nest into a skin and flung it with a flexible pole. The noise of the enraged hornet's sounded like enemy war cries.

The Norsemen retreated in disarray at this unexpected turn of events.

157

One of them, however, stood her ground. Freydis, the powerful daughter of Erik the Red, picked up a sword of a fallen countryman and challenged their advance. In good Viking style, she slapped the weapon against her bared breast with such a gesture of defiance that it was now the Skraeling's turn to flee to their boats. It was not easy for these Norsemen to be put to shame by a woman. So they claimed that the enemy's secret weapon came from a supernatural power.

Not everything they reported is easy for us to believe. One of these stories is about a "uniped," a one-legged man who kept following them on shore but escaped their chase. They believed that he had slain Leif's brother Thorvald.

Returning to Greenland and then to Iceland with a cargo of wood and furs made Thorfinn an even richer man. It also inspired many more young men to travel to Vinland. According to the "Greenlander's Saga," after Thorfinn died and his son was married, Gudrid travelled to Rome and joined a convent.

CHAPTER 75

The Vinland
Map

T
HE VINLAND MAP, published by Yale University in 1965, has been the most controversial item of Scandinavian discussion in this century. The map was drawn on a folded, single sheet of vellum, 11 by 16 inches, and was believed to have dated from about 1440, 50 years before Columbus made his "discovery" of America. It was featured on the cover of the Journal of the American Medical Association in 1969, with a story called "The Vinland Map and the Tartar Relation."

For about a decade, this map attracted an immense amount of serious curiosity. But even though Yale University is one of the most prestigious centers of learning in the world, not all scholars were convinced of its authenticity. Two of them, Gwyn Jones and Magnus Magnusson, have written about their doubts of the document. Jones is a noted Celtic scholar from Cardiff, England, and Magnusson is a native of Iceland, now living in Scotland, who produced the PBS-TV series, "Vikings!" Magnusson had been an early enthusiast for the Vinland Map.

O. G. Landsverk, an American scientist of Scandinavian descent, suggested that the map had been drawn up in connection with a church council at Basle, Switzerland, in 1440. He noted the surprising accuracy of the map and concluded that Scandinavians had supplied the information on North America. It also bears resemblance to a map drawn in 1436 by Andrea Bianco, a Venetian cartographer.

How did Yale University obtain this mysterious map and what was the "Tartar Relation?" An Italian bookseller living in Barcelona had shown it to booksellers in Geneva, London and Paris. It was bound together with a previously unknown story about the mission of a Franciscan missionary to the Mongol Court in 1245-47. As predictable, the experts in the British Museum were skeptical and rejected it.

An American antiquarian dealer purchased the map in Geneva for $3500, quite convinced that it was genuine. Two problems caused the

Yale scholars to hesitate. First, it was bound in a modern volume; and second, some worm holes in the map did not correspond between the two folded parts. It was also drawn a little too accurately for its time. In 1959, a friend of Yale purchased the map for about $400,000 and donated it to the University.

Magnusson describes his conclusions about the map in his book, "Vikings!" (1980). The final test was a micro-analytical examination of the ink. The ink used in the map showing the "Tartar Relation" was an organic iron gallotannate, common to the Middle Ages. The ink used for drawing the New World contained an inorganic element called titanium dioxide which was not developed until 1917. On January 26, 1974, Yale University issued this statement, "researches suggest that the famous Vinland Map may be a forgery."

Does this discredit the Norse claim to have discovered "Vinland?" Not at all. It does show that the cartographer, whoever he was and whenever he lived, had studied the Vinland Sagas. The map would have been unique for there is no other evidence of Norse sailors making or using maps and charts. Prof. Jones wrote his first edition of "A History of the Vikings" in 1968 and, while cautious about the map, nevertheless held out interesting speculations about its significance if proven authentic. His revised edition of 1984 refers to it as a "discredited forgery."

Since the Yale statement in 1974, the map has not been taken seriously by most scholars, though a mountain of circumstantial evidence had been assembled. Despite this consensus, Dr. Landsverk, a nuclear physicist, has some powerful arguments in defense of the map's authenticity. It would be ironic if Yale's denial was premature. (See Chapter 77.)

How did the Norsemen travel? Like other ancient mariners, they followed the ocean currents and took their directions from the sun and stars. Their single sails did not tack against the wind, as later sailing vessels did. This is why many of them were lost at sea and never made it to their destinations. Those who did arrive and return were the lucky ones. Their navigation information was handed down through "oral tradition," with a degree of secrecy to protect their "thing" from being exploited by others.

There is also disagreement about how long the Norse voyages from

Greenland to Vinland were continued. Jones thinks that they were suspended after 1020. This is hard to know for sure since the sagas and other records indicate that they continued for another century. What is known for sure is that the Norsemen lost interest in setting up colonies in a land occupied by hostile natives. Greenland didn't have that many people to spare.

This reluctance to warfare offers a different insight to our understanding of the Norsemen. They have been pictured as blood thirsty and lusty buccaneers who got their kicks from looting and killing. Like other pagans (and some Christians too), they could be incited to wars of conquests (compare the Crusades!). Like other people, Norsemen loved their families and were simply trying to provide homes and opportunities for them. Part of their problem has been bad press. It was mostly their enemies who wrote about them. Modern media has exploited this. When we lived in Chicago, our son Daniel was in a scuffle with a neighborhood boy who asked what nationality he was. Dan answered, "Viking," and the other boy promptly withdrew from the fight. He'd been watching the movies.

CHAPTER 76

Norse Rune Stones
In America

NOT EVERYONE HAS AGREED with those who delcared the Vinland Map a forgery. One of these was Dr. O. G. Landsverk, a Norwegian-American scientist and former nuclear physicist with a Ph. D. from the University of Chicago. He collaborated with Alf Monge, a former cryptanalyst with the United States Army Intelligence.

If I had any doubts of the competence about these scholars, I was reassured by Prof. H. M. Blegen of Augustana College, Sioux Falls, SD, who has written of them with high praise. Since I've had the greatest respect for Dr. Blegen, I've studied the work of these two scholars with special interest. When Yale University issued its statement in 1974 suggesting that the Vinland Map may be a forgery, Landsverk claimed the tests to be faulty on which the conclusions were based.

Landsverk's book, "Runic Records of the Norsemen in America," is impressive. His data compares runic writings found in the Orkney Islands, Greenland, New England, Minnesota, Illinois, the Dakotas and Oklahoma. He credits Alf Monge, a specialist in decoding messages for the Army, with having discovered the secret to understanding the runic messages. They note, however, that not all runic writings contain these cryptic insertions.

The Norse presence on the North American continent has been tied to their existence in Greenland from 986 to 1500 A.D. An abundance of Norse artifacts have been found in the New World, but there has been a deep-seated resistance to accept them as evidence. The work of Landsverk and Monge claims to have discovered hidden dates in them from the "Primstav," the perpetual church calendar of the Middle Ages. (See chapter 35.) The announcement of this discovery was made in 1967. I'm not aware that anyone has successfully challenged their claim.

Landsverk was convinced that the Kensington Stone found near Alexandria, Minnesota, which claims to date from 1362, is authentic. He also claims that bones excavated in 1905 from Mandan Indian sites north of Bismarck, ND, have Norse runic inscriptions. Some of these are on display at the Peabody Museum at Harvard University, some at the Smithsonian Institute and three are at the Ft. Lincoln Memorial Museum at Mandan, ND. These finds become especially interesting in the light of Verendrye's observation in 1738 that the Mandan Indians had many European characteristics.

What were those Norsemen doing in Midwest America 500 years before Columbus? Landsverk claims that the ship carrying the "8 Goths and 22 Norwegians," which travelled to Kensington, set sail from Bergen in 1355 by order of King Magnus "to find and bring back to the true faith the Norse Greenlanders who had abandoned their homes in Greenland" and settled on the American continent. He was supported in this theory by the late Hjalmar Rued Holand, professor at the University of Wisconsin.

But how do the runic writings fit into this story? Runic, a form of writing carved into rocks and wood, was used by the Norsemen before Christianity and the Latin took over about 1000. Runic, sometimes called "futhark," continued to survive among the Runemasters, chiefly clergy, who used it to inscribe coded messages.

The runes expressed numbers as well as sounds, according to Landsverk. The Primstav was used by the Norse puzzlemasters who kept on using their runic writing long after it was considered "unchristian" to do so. It's interesting that it was the Norse clergy who became the experts in writing secret messages with runic inscriptions. As a result Norwegian and Swedish churches of the Middle Ages are decorated with runic writings. The Scandinavian church, having originated through England instead of the Continent, seems to have been permitted this deviation from church practice until about 1350 to assure loyalty to Rome. The Norse clergy retained the spirit of freedom which was part of their ancient tradition, a trait still inherent in Norwegian-Americans today. In the 17th century, runes were identified with magic and many people were put to death in Iceland just for having knowledge of them.

The stave church from Gol in Hallingdal was brought to the Folk Museum at Bygdoy Park near Oslo in 1885 with the help of King Oscar II. It has 13 runic inscriptions. Early attempts to read them proved difficult until Alf Monge's work of deciphering. For a while, scholars had thought them to have been done by amateur writers. Not only stave churches, but Nidarosdomen, Norway's national cathedral in Trondheim, has 40 runic puzzles.

Many reports on the Kensingston Stone have commented on its "bad Latin." Later cryptanalysis by Monge claims them to be the evidence of Norse puzzlemasters. The Kensington Stone was discovered in 1898 by Olaf Ohman, a Swedish farmer. Magnus Magnusson, creator the popular "Vikings!" PBS-TV series, has called it a "forgery," together with the Vinland Map. His arguments sound convincing. But I have two reasons, neither of them scientific, for thinking that the Kensington Stone may be for real. First, those Norsemen from the Middle Ages were resourceful travellers. Second, there's a snobbery on the part of many Europeans which is reluctant to admit that anything of importance has happened in the New World. It's still a British inuendo to regard the United States as one of the "colonies."

CHAPTER 77

Immigrants From
Voss To America

I S THERE ANY PLACE IN NORWAY that did not pour out its people to come to America? Not since the Black Death of 1349 did Norway lose so many of its people as in the emigrations of the 19th century. Only Ireland contributed a larger percent of its population to the New World.

The city of Voss is one of the beauty spots in Norway's "Westlands." Its scenery is captivating and people delightful. The clean shops, the lovely Vangskyrkja (the church) and the landscape exposure to the south make it an ideal place to vacation. The church was built in 1277. Before 1840, there were less than three miles of good roads in the entire district. Not until 1883, when the railroad from Bergen was built, did Voss get a solid connection with the outside world, shortening the travel time between those two points from one week to four hours. Today there is excellent rail and highway travel from Oslo as well.

While "Vossings" have settled in all parts of America, the two largest concentrations have been Koshkonong, near Madison, Wisconsin, and Chicago, a city of only 4000 people when the first Vossings arrived in 1836. (See Odd S. Louoll's book "A Century of Urban Life: The Norwegians in Chicago Before 1930" - 1988.) I became acquainted with many of them when living in the "Windy City." The first Norwegian club in America was organized in 1848 by Vossings in Chicago who promoted correspondence with Norway.

Two people for whom Voss is especially dear, Jonas and Mabel Wold of Minot, North Dakota, have shared with me a book telling of its emigration, entitled "Gammalt Fra Voss," ("Old Times from Voss"), written in both Norwegian and English.

Voss offered only a meager living from the soil for its people until the 1930s. When the population started to increase greatly during the middle 18th century, people broke up more land for farming. Most of these were "crofters," or "cotters" who lived on small plots on the edge

165

of the main farms of the valleys.

Despite its remoteness, Voss was known for having a high level of industry and ingenuity. Ivar Aasen (1813-1896), whose statue stands on the campus of Concordia College in Moorhead, Minnesota, and one of Norway's greatest educators, wrote of Voss: "Here you meet not only ordinary craftsmen and journeymen but also distinguished draftsmen and signet-engravers, clockmakers and even organ builders." Though largely self-taught, this community was also lucid in its usage of language and grammar. Voss has had one poet of unusual talent, Per Sivle (1857-1904). He is not well known in America, but is recognized in Norway as one of its great writers. There's a Sons of Norway lodge at Simco, North Dakota, named after Sivle.

People started leaving Voss by 1750 for northern Norway. It was not until 1836 that organized movements left for America. The most famous Vossing to come to America was Knute Rockne (1888-1931), the great football coach at Notre Dame University. The Rocknes were one of the oldest families in the village and were famed for their skill as blacksmiths and carriage makers. Knute's father, Lars, won second prize at the 1891 Chicago World's Fair with his one-horse carriage. Two years later, when Knute was only five, he sent for his family. He grew up in the heavily Scandinavian northwest side of Chicago. I had my internship in that community in 1950-1951 and found many people who still remembered Rockne. His pastor said that Knute never forgot him at Christmas, even after he had become famous. A monument honoring Rockne has been erected in Voss, near his birthplace.

Elling Eielsen (1804-1883), who came from Voss as a lay preacher, had a strong impact on the early Norwegian communities in America. His family was influenced by Hans Nielsen Hauge, the farmer who brought a religious revival to Norway that has left a permanent effect on its people. He founded the "Evangelical Lutheran Church in America," known as the "Eielsen Synod." This is the same name chosen for the 1988 merger of the largest denomination of Lutherans in America.

Voss was also noted for politicians in America. The most famous of these was Knute Nelson (1842-1923). After the Civil War, he got a law degree and bought a farm near Alexandria, Minnesota. Elected to Congress in 1883, he became the first Norwegian-born American governor in 1892. In 1895, he was elected the first Scandinavian-born United States senator and served in that post until his death in 1923. Erling Rolfsrud has written a delightful little book on Nelson named "Scandinavian Moses."

Ragnvald Nestos (1877-1942) emigrated from Voss with his parents to North Dakota at age 16. After homesteading in Pierce County, he studied law at the University of North Dakota and went into partnership with C. A. Johnson and O. B. Herigstad in Minot. A political conservative, Nestos was elected in 1910 to the state legislature. He was instrumental in obtaining the initial appropriation for the first building at Minot State University and helped secure funding for Minot's first public library. When Lynn Frazier was recalled in 1921, Nestos was elected governor of North Dakota and served until 1924. In 1925, he was a delegate to the League of Nations and was the General Chairman for the visit of Crown Prince Olav and Crown Princess Martha when they visited Minot in 1939. Nestos was inducted into the Scandinavian-American Hall of Fame by the Norsk Høstfest on October 24, 1986. He was also a founder and first president of Minot's Sons of Norway Thor Lodge 67 in 1907.

Though a community of about only 10,000, the people of Voss have been faithful to the best in the Scandinavian heritage and have become a reason for pride among all Americans.

CHAPTER 78

Scandinavia And The 'Northern Crusades'

THE CRUSADES OF THE MIDDLE AGES conjure up images of knights in armor, pious kings, saints who see visions and even little children marching to Jerusalem to free the "Holy Land" from the "Infidel." It was this, but not all the marching was to the Middle East. There were also crusades to the Baltic regions of northern Europe to convert the heathen. There was no similar attempt to convert the Moslems.

The word "crusade" means to "mark with the cross." When a king or knight "took the cross," it was a solemn pledge to spend his money and even give his life to free Palestine from the Moslems or to convert the pagans of eastern Europe. It involved a solemn and binding ceremony. One of the most interesting of these kings was Louis IX (1226-1270) of France, known as "St. Louis" and who has a major American city named after him.

Compared to the expeditions to the Middle East, the crusades of the North are little known. Among the most active participants were the kings of Denmark, especially Valdemar the Great (1157-1182) and his successors, who took delight in going after unbelievers. He was aided by his foster brother, Archbishop Absalon, the founder of Copenhagen, whose statue stands proudly in that city today.

To be properly called a "crusade" or "holy war," the military expedition had to be authorized by the church leaders in Rome. From the religious point of view, the missionary efforts to conquor the unbelievers carried full remission of sins to those who "took up the cross." The first of these northern crusades was ordered in 1147 and the last was in 1505. While the crusades of the North were not as spectacular as those in the Mediterranean, they were less costly and brought about more lasting changes.

The invaded territories included Prussia, Livonia, Estonia, Lithuania and Finland. In 1240, a crusade was directed against the Orthodox

Christian areas of Russia, but was repulsed. The Swedes and Saxons also joined the crusades. Several orders of Knights were involved. The Teutonic Knights, Prussian Knights and the Brothers of the Sword (an army of monks) shared the fame of these holy wars.

Denmark was a leader in the crusades because of its naval strength. In 1100, the Danes could put to sea a fleet of 860 ships. The war-like spirit of the Vikings was not quickly extinguished from the souls of these Norsemen, even though they had officially adopted the Christian faith. Fighting was still in their blood. It was not that Valdemar and the other Scandinavian kings were so "religious," the crusades were an outlet for that love of battle which had been their way of life for centuries. There was also the opportunity to gain territory, because they could occupy the lands they conquered and tax its income after the people had been baptized. Eric Christiansen, professor of history at Oxford University, writes: "The Scandinavians had accepted Christ without rejecting their ancestral values."

Among the preachers who urged the crusades was St. Bernard of Clairvaux (1091-1153), a Cistercian monk revered to this day by both Roman Catholics and Protestants for his piety. The adventurous Scandinavians were not slow to accept his challenge to fight the heathen "until such a time as, by God's help, they shall be either converted or wiped out." Baptism or death were the alternatives.

Danes get a patriotic chill from hearing the story of how Denmark got its flag, the "Dannebrog." It comes from one of these crusading wars led by King Valdemar II (1202-1241). In the battle of Lyndaniz against the Estonians on June 15, 1219, the Danes were losing when a red banner with a white cross was said to have dropped miraculously from the sky and turned defeat into victory. The Danish army adopted the banner and to this day it flies at nearly every home in Denmark (and in my house too). Now you know what an army from Denmark was doing in Estonia.

The Finns were conquered through a crusade led by Sweden's King Eric IX (St. Eric). He was accompanied in battle by Bishop Henry of Uppsala who was later martyred and is known to us today as "St. Henry." He had originally come from England. One of Stockholm's most famous names is Birger Jarl. No visitor to Sweden's capital city can miss it. He led an expedition against the unbelieving Finns in 1249 "because he wanted to increase his fame" and God's.

One of the last major battles of the northern crusades was at Tannenberg in Prussia on July 15, 1410, where the Teutonic Knights suffered a crushing defeat. It was the same place that the Czar's army suffered a devasting debacle on August 20, 1914, at the hands of the Kaiser's troops. The people grew tired of crusades and did not respond for the call to march against the heathen. What did the knights do when they ran out of wars in Europe? They become "Conquistadors" and continued the "holy war" against the heathen Aztecs and Incas of the New World.

The crusades, however, were big business in those days and the economy of many communities thrived as ships were built, swords were forged and supplies laid in for these wars fought for the honor of God's name. It is supposed that we have become wiser from these events of the past. But the longer I live, the more amazed I am at our preoccupation with "warring madness." How many more thousands of years will it take before we learn?

CHAPTER 79

Jon Wefald —
Kansas State Prexy

JON WEFALD IS A MAN WHO LIKES challenges. Half way through his freshman year at Pacific Lutheran University in Tacoma, Washington, he discovered that he had the ability to excel. He's been doing it ever since. From there he went to Washington State University in Pullman for a master's degree (1961) and to the University of Michigan at Ann Arbor for a doctorate (1965). His field of study has been history and political science. On July 1, 1986, he became president of Kansas State University at Manhattan.

Wefald is described as "a man with a vision" by Beth Hartenstein, writing for the "K-Stater," the official bulletin of the University. After teaching at Gustavus Adolphus College in St. Peter, Minn. (1965-1970), and serving for six years as Commissioner of Agriculture in Minnesota, Welfald became President of Southwest State University in Marshall in 1977. There were those who thought the institution's problems were beyond solving, including former Governor Wendell Anderson. During his first year at the helm, Wefald visited more than 80 high schools. Enrollment rose 56 percent that fall.

He did his job so well that after five years he was appointed Chancellor of the Minnesota State University System, consisting of seven state universities which also were deep in problems. In Minnesota, Wefald was at the head of 51,000 students with a biennial budget of $354 million dollars, in contrast to Kansas State, which has 18,000 students and a budget of $183 million. He went to K-State because he believed it is an excellent university with an enormous potential.

Welfald has set some high goals. "I want to make Kansas the leading education state in America. I'd like to see the goal of Kansas becoming one of the very top brain power states." He intends to focus on academic and athletic excellence and hopes to make K-State one of "the top two or three schools in the Big Eight and one of the top 15 (out of 69) land grant schools in the nation." K-State was one of the four finalists in

171

NCAA basketball in 1988, losing out to the University of Kansas Jay Hawks in the semifinals.

Welfald didn't waste any time launching into his new Kansas career. Even before moving into the President's office, he announced that eight additional admissions counselors would be appointed to increase and stabilize the enrollment. He is challenging the University's alumni to recruit one student each year.

The secret of Welfald's success has been his collegial style of teamwork. Former Governor Anderson stated that he brought cooperation and unity to the Minnesota State University System. At his farewell dinner, testimonials described him as having "brought a great deal of harmony to the workplace, created an ability to work together as a team for a common cause and goal. He can instill that sense of everyone working together. He brings out the best in the people he works with, and he's not afraid of people who are very strong."

That's pretty good for a boy who grew up as an average student in the Minot, North Dakota, school system and the son of a grain inspector. Wefald's Norwegian ancestry may have had some influence on his commitment to the work ethic. He thrives on hard work, but his friends claim he has a good sense of humor that turns work into a pleasure rather than a drudgery. He combines his love for humanity with the ability to articulate ideas clearly.

Why did K-State turn to the Chancellor of the Minnesota State University System in its search for a new president? According to Regent Richard Reinhardt, Wefald's selection was a "statement of direction for Kansas State University." His background as a Chancellor of state universities in Minnesota and as state Commissioner of Agriculture seemed to be just what the regents wanted for Kansas. They also took note of his reputation as a team leader and his success as an administration builder.

Kansas State University has had many reknowned presidents, including Milton Eisenhower. Wefald is the 12th president. Among the early and colorful leaders was John Alexander Anderson, who had come from a long line of Scottish Presbyterian ministers. He not only shaped the university, but left his mark on "every feature of the development of Kansas" and went on to serve six terms in Congress. Jon Wefald has his work cut out for him and it's my guess that he will bring new heights to K-State from his office in Anderson Hall.

Wefald's influence has not been limited to the campus. He has been a speaker for many conferences and TV appearances throughout the nation, besides being a published author. The year before going to Kansas, Minnesota Governor Rudy Perpich appointed him Chairman of the newly proposed State-wide High School for the Arts. He's received many honors from government, corporations, universities, the Jaycees and Future Farmers of America. He gave the commencement address at Minot State University in 1987 and held the audience's complete attention throughout.

Like Americans from many ethnic backgrounds, the Norwegian-American Wefald has has come a long way. Once these people were the terror of monasteries which kept learning alive in the Middle Ages. Today Scandinavians have a reputation for highly respecting education. Dr. Jon Wefald does America proud by his Scandinavian heritage.

*President
Jon Wefald -
Kansas State
University.*

CHAPTER 80

Slaves And Free Men In The Viking World

EVERY MAN KNEW HIS PLACE in the Viking world. It was a society with firmly fixed class distinctions rooted in religious mythology. The Icelandic myth, "Voluspa," named the god "Heimdall" as the father of men in their different classes. Their rank depended on who was their mother. Norwegians of today are indebted to the Icelandic poets for preserving both their mythologies and earliest histories. Since most of the original Icelanders were immigrants from Norway, they became the recorders of the tradition, just like ethnic Norwegians in America celebrate their heritage more than their cousins in the homelands.

Heimdall's three sons were named Thrall (slave), Karl (a free independent farmer) and Jarl (an "Earl," born to be a ruler). The youngest of Jarl's sons was named Konr, from which the name "king" (konungr) derived. The king represents the top of the social ladder.

The Karls and the Jarls got their slaves through raiding and trading. Slave trade was big business among Vikings. They seized people on raids of Scandinavia as well as surrounding countries. The largest number seems to have been obtained in Ireland. People had an eye for profit and were not unwilling to sell their fellow countrymen. Securing wealth was the main motive for the business. They were no different than Joseph's brothers in Palestine.

Slaves seized through raiding were often held as hostages for ransom, if they happened to come from a wealthy family. Kidnapping was a popular sport in the ancient world. Ransoming "hostages" was one of the incentives for Christian missions. It wasn't only the Vikings who did this. St. Patrick, born of Roman ancestry in England, was kidnapped by Irish pirates and forcibly taken to the Emerald Island. After getting free and spending time on the Continent, he returned as a missionary to the people who once held him captive. It was not unusual for the bishop to sell the altar vessels in order to "redeem" a kidnapped

Christian. In 1012, the Danes held as hostage Aelfeah, the Archbishop of Canterbury. He refused to allow anyone to ransom him, so his captors crushed his skull with an axe. Slave markets flourished in the Middle Ages. Raiders from Germany carried off 700 Danes in 1169 and these all appeared on the market in one day of traiding at Mecklenburg.

Slaves had the lowest of legal positions and very few rights. They were regarded as chattel, like cattle. They could own nothing, inherit nothing and their marriages had no standing. Their children were the property of their masters. They had no vote in public assemblies ("Things") or in the military. The laws governing the status of slaves varied from place to place, but not a great deal.

When Christianity came to Scandinavia, slaves were baptized, confirmed and given Christian rites and burial. The church taught that their place in the afterworld did not depend on their position in this world. According to St. Paul that there was no difference between slave and free. Christianity softened the treatment of slaves, but it did not gain their freedom quickly. There was no civil war in Scandinavia to free the slaves.

The number of slaves was controlled by killing the old and infirm and by exposing their infants to die. Sacredness of life was only slowly extended to slaves through the influence of the church.

How could a slave become free? In the Trondheim area, it was the custom to free one slave each year as an act of piety. In Sweden, it became a crime to sell a Christian slave. This resulted in automatic freedom. Sometimes an owner rewarded a slave with freedom for his services. In case of an invasion, a slave who killed an enemy was made free. Slaves sometimes were allowed to earn money, like prisoners, and they could buy their freedom.

A "freedom feast" was a required legal formality and a social ceremony. A slave was not fully free until this event took place. The laws of the local assemblies carefully prescribed the procedures for these events. Even after gaining freedom, the slave often had some obligations to his former master and it was not until the fifth generation in Trondelag that the descendants had the full status as "freedmen." If the freedman should turn against his former master during this probation period, it could result in reverting to full slavery again. There were also laws governing the status of children born to a slaveowner by a slave mother.

The children of slaves were given demeaning names such as Laggard, Barn-man, Beaked-nose, Clump, etc. Slaves were easy to identify by their simple undyed clothing and their close-cropped hair. They did the difficult tasks on the farm as a true Viking thought of work as beneath his dignity. Slaves were despised and considered unreliable, stupid, foul and cowardly.

The life of the slave was always hard and uncertain. When freedom finally came to the slaves sometime in the 13th century, they often became cotters, living on marginal lands and still having to perform duties to the main landower. It was finally the "Black Death" that ended the vestiges of slavery. Up to half or more of the people of Scandinavia died from the Bubonic Plague. This made land easily available and workers scarce.

The path to freedom in all lands has been slow and difficult. The price paid for it must never be forgotten by the children who have inherited it without cost.

CHAPTER 81

The Political Views
Of Norwegian Immigrants

EW IMMIGRANTS WERE SO prepared to participate in the democratic process as those from Norway. Since 1814, Norwegians had come alive to their right to be free people. That was the year when Denmark was forced to sign Norway over to the King of Sweden in the Treaty of Kiel because it had reluctantly entered the continental wars on the side of Napoleon.

The Norwegians immediately called a constitutional convention at Eidsvoll on April 10 and had a document ready to sign on May 17 ("syttende Mai"), modeled on the new American and French constitutions. Napoleon's Marshall Bernadotte, who had recently become Crown Prince Karl Johan of Sweden, invaded Norway and put a stop to secession.

Having gotten that close to independence, the ancient spirit of the Norse free assemblies ("Things") came to life. While it took another 91 years (three generations) to gain their full freedom, these immigrants to America were dedicated to democracy. Even in the darkest days of the Middle Ages, the farmers of Norway and Sweden never lost their freedom, though they had to battle kings, nobles and bishops to retain it.

While conservative in their personal economy, the Norse immigrants were usually to the left of center in their political views. An excellent book on this subject is "A Voice of Protest," by Dr. Jon Wefald, based on his doctoral dissertation at the University of Michigan, published by the Norwegian-American Historical Association (1971).

The Norwegians were different from many of their "Yankee" neighbors or most of the other European immigrants, who were politically conservatve. The Norwegians brought with them a deep feeling of community and challenged the capitalistic exploitations which they experienced when entering the job market in America. They didn't buy into the myths of Horatio Alger's success story, social Darwinism

177

and laissez faire ("hands-off") economic theories. They favored govern-ment regulations to curb the unbridled greed of capitalism and wanted the producer and consumer in closer contact, eliminating middlemen.

While the dream of establishing a "Little Norway" was not to be, they were highly successful in politics. They broke with the Democrats over the slavery issue in the Civil War and generally voted with progressive Republicans who promised free soil, free speech and free men. Norwe-gian immigrants liked Teddy Roosevelt, Populism and cooperatives. Their definition of a "Yankee" was someone who'd cheat you out of your last cent and refuse a night of lodging when you were broke.

As foreigners, the Norwegian immigrants faced discrimination in the job market and in elections. But it wasn't long before they banded together and a Norwegian name became a political asset. They were accustomed to political debates from their homeland. One of their heroes was Johan Sverdrup (1816-1892), leader of Norway's Liberal Par-ty in its campaign for freedom during the Swedish period (1814-1905). His grandfather had been president of the Constitutional Convention. It was natural for Scandinavian immigrants to participate in local civic affairs, unlike most other Europeans.

By 1889, the year that North Dakota became a state, Norwegian im-migrants won the majority of the best offices in Trail County. By 1905, they occupied 2000 county offices in America. State and national posi-tions were not long in coming. Knute Nelson of Minnesota attacked the American industrialists, including big banks, corporations and labor unions. He was the first Norse immigrant to become a governor and served in both the U.S. House and Senate. Andrew Lee was a Norwegian Populist governor in South Dakota. Karl Rolvaag wrote about Populism in "Their Father's God." I get the feeling that he admired the idealism of Populism but didn't think it would work.

Resentment rose against the Norwegians for their aggressive pursuit of public office. The Mayville Tribune attacked the Scandinavian Republican league, saying it was "entirely foreign to Americanism." It complained that "the Scandinavian element all over North Dakota to-day (1889) has three-fourths of the best offices in nearly every coun-ty." The Minneapolis and St. Paul papers joined in the protest. In 1907, 30 Norwegian-born Americans were in the North Dakota House of

Representatives. The state capitol buzzed with the Norse language. Five Norwegians served on the railroad commission between 1900 and 1907. In Wisconsin, the Norwegians found Robert M. La Follette to their liking, but elected one of their own, James Davidson, to succeed him as governor.

The Norwegians brought with them a "socialism" based on rural values imbued with Christian ideals which favored equitable distribution of wealth. It was not to be compared with Marxist socialism and determinism. They were oriented to protest and reform, especially in North Dakota where they brought radicalism, according to historian Elwyn B. Robinson. The Nonpartisan League would not have happened without the Norwegian immigrants. They were passionately loyal to America. It was well expressed by Congressman Gilbert Haugen of Iowa: "Every's man's duty . . . is to strive to benefit this country, protect the weak, relieve the distressed, uplift humanity." This was their dream for the New World, and the dream lives on.

CHAPTER 82

The Norwegian
Immigrant Press

ABOUT 400 NORWEGIAN LANGUAGE newspapers were started in America. Almost every immigrant family subscribed to one or more. What accounted for this eagerness to read? Strange as it may seem, the reason was a law made by the King of Denmark on Feb. 25, 1720, requiring public catechization of youth every Sunday between Easter and Michaelmas (Sept. 29). The strong emphasis on confirmation required that every young person could read. This made Denmark and Norway some of the most literate countries in the world.

Svein Nilsson (1826-1908) was an early Norwegian editor in America. He published Billed Magazin ("picture magazine") in Madison, Wisconsin, from 1868-1870. It was generations ahead of "Life" and "Look" magazines and sold for $1.00 a year or two cents an issue.

In 1870, Nilsson went to Chicago where he was editor-in-chief of the Scandinavin until 1886. Scandinavin, established in 1866, was a liberal Republican paper which became the most influential molder of opinion among Norwegian immigrants. Its sympathy was for the "common man" and it became a crusader for public schools. It opposed the Norwegian Lutheran Synod practice of establishing parochial schools.

It was in politics, however, that the Norwegian immigrant press found its focus. The immigrants held to their democratic rural values and were surprised when America didn't turn out to be what the advertisements claimed. They had been duped by the travel agents who sold them tickets to a land where they could expect to get rich quick.

The early Norwegian settlers earned a reputation for being "independent." They preferred to live on farms where they could be their own bosses, rather than in factories. The Yankee establishment was charged with caring more for their mules than their laborers, since mules cost money but workers were free. They started their newspapers as a voice of protest for social reform. Their ancient spirit of freedom would not die in the new land. Through their press, they attacked the Yankee philosophy of "rugged individualism" which grew rich on exploiting immigrants.

In North Dakota, the Normanden (1887-1954), published in Grand Forks, became the most influential Norwegian newspaper in the state. It began as an advocate for Populist views, but switched to being progressive Republican when the Fram in Fargo became the Norwegian voice of the Nonpartison League. The Red River Valley was the center of the Norse immigrant press. Fargo had the most newspapers. Some of the other cities with influential newspapers were Enderlin, Portland and Hillsboro in North Dakota. Minneapolis and Fergus Falls in Minnesota, Sioux Falls, South Dakota, and Decorah, Iowa, were just a few of the other cities to have influential Norwegian newspapers.

The Norwegian and Yankee newspapers fought a continual battle over social issues. The Yankee writers charged that the unemployed were "tramps" and that the answer to poverty was to work harder. The Norwegians responded by accusing the bankers of greed. They urged Chicago meatpacker Jonathon Armour to set up a pension fund for his workers. While the Norwegians often disagreed with the labor union bosses who denied them jobs, they championed the cause of the labor movement. They claimed the answer was not "minimum wages," but "maximum wages" for a worker's toil. They challenged the employer to pay the worker the highest possible wages for work, not the least with which they could get away.

When the World War of 1914 came, the Norwegian press and congressmen stuck with the "neutralism" of their homeland and opposed President Wilson's pro-English policies. As a result, Norwegian-Americans were often charged with being "pro-German." This, unfortunately, happened to our family. Some Yankee school kids taunted my father as being "pro-German." A witness told me years later that this was the only time they had ever seen him angry. His oldest brother had been killed in France just a few weeks earlier. The Secret Service kept close watch on Dr. Markus Bockman, president of Luther Theological Seminary in St. Paul, during the war years. A great biblical scholar, he lectured only in Norwegian. The government agents supposed that he was supporting the Kaiser's cause.

Most Norwegian-American congressmen voted against Wilson's request for declaration of war on Germany. Senator Asle Gronna of North Dakota said, "I shall vote against war because I believe it would have been possible to maintain an honorable peace with all the nations of the earth . . . I am opposed to war because war means destruction, misery, and poverty to the toiling millions of our country for generations to come." A poll was taken in 1939 among Norwegian-Americans in which 105 out of 121 said they had opposed the war. Their common view held it to be a "money-man's war." I remember Dr. Iver Iverson, a history professor, tell us with a twinkle in his eye that America had been assured that we would not get into Europe's war because "the bankers won't allow it." The tables have now turned and the sons of the immigrants have become prominent bankers, but I can remember when the banker and the sheriff were feared among immigrant families, just as they had been in Norway.

Even though separated by a vast ocean from their homeland, the immigrants retained the humanitarian values of social justice learned in the old country. Their press was largely responsible for this. Today only three Norwegian language newspapers survive. They're located in Brooklyn, Chicago and Seattle. But they belong to a proud heritage.

CHAPTER **83**

Family Life In
The Viking World

WHEN THE NORSEMEN WERE OUT "viking" (raiding),
somebody had to stay home and take care of the farms
and families. The summer farm work fell to old men,
women, slaves and children. It was especially the wom-
en, however, who managed such tasks. The perils of sea travel and the
loss of life in war resulted in a shortage of men back home. When the
men returned, they'd repair their boats and weapons, and spend the
long, dark winter nights drinking ale, telling of their exploits and planning their next year's expeditions.

A popular misconception of the Viking Age is that it was a glamorous
time. It's true that men sometimes brought home expensive jewelry for
their wives which was proudly displayed, but for the most part life was
glum and lacking in security. The Vikings also raided each others home
and left a trail of burned buildings and blood. Like all pagans, they lived
in fear of fickle gods. Fatalism and determinism dominated their view
of life.

Women did not have the customary rights that we take for granted
in the western world today, but a strong minded woman did exercise
influence in everyday decision making. Women's work was caring for
children, serving food, milking cows, making cloth and clothes, washing
laundry and needle work. The famous Hardanger stitches are not a
modern innovation. It represents a long tradition of skill practiced by
Norse women.

Women had no political rights and only limited benefits of in-
heritance. Unmarried women were kept under the guardianship of their
families. Widows, however, could manage their own homes. Daughters
were regarded as the property of the family and were guarded jealously.
A broken engagement could result in blood-vengeance. Writing love
poems in Iceland was forbidden. But as usual, what was banned was
also popular.

With few exceptions, people stayed in their own social class. A rich man would not give his daughter to a poor suitor. "Matchmakers" might act as brokers between guardians and prospective grooms. It could lead to a lot of haggling. The wedding was not legal and the children not legitimate until the "bride price" was paid by the groom. In Norway, a minimum of 12 ounces of silver was required and that was called "the poor man's price." The groom was expected to add a percentage to the dowery after the ceremony. The bride's consent for marriage was not required. In Christian times, however, an unwilling bride could get out of a marriage by going to a convent and becoming a nun.

At the husbands's discretion, adultery was punishable with death for a woman, while men were not penalized for extramarital activities. Divorce was uncommon. Wives usually stuck by their husbands even when it meant death. In the Icelandic saga of Njal, his wife refused to leave their burning farmhouse (set fire by his enemies), saying: "I was given young to Njal, and I have promised him that one fate shall fall on us both."

Population control dictated that the old and feeble were allowed to die. When a child was born, the father made the decision whether it should live or be exposed to death. Legitimate children had a better chance of survival. Illegitimate births were high risk and the deformed almost certain to perish. But once a child had been nursed at its mother's breast, life was guaranteed. Property rights were jealously guarded and were reserved for the wanted. Presents were given when the first tooth was cut and when a person became of age at 15 or 16.

The handicapped and destitute were the responsibility of the family. The coming of Christianity, with its emphasis on "good works," made charity a responsibility of the community. But it took centuries for these social improvements to take effect. The introduction of the tithe by the church and food saved from fasting made possible both relief work and the building of hospitals.

Iceland developed a mutual insurance plan to help the unfortunate. If a farmer lost a quarter or more of his cattle through disease, his neighbors would make good the loss. The same was true if a farmstead lost three or more of its buildings through fire. Such contributions were limited to 1% of total income and no one could receive insurance compensation more three times.

Despite the harshness of life, Scandinavia was not a worse place to live than other countries. On the contrary, even in the heathen days, loyalty to family was an obligation. Our later times have eroded much of that sense of duty and self reliance. It was not until the last 100 years or so that the great social reforms have taken place. The challenge of such support systems for us is to maintain visible signs of family loyalty.

Some of the ancient qualities still persist among Scandinavians. It was the custom of families to take care of their own handicapped, feeble minded and illegitimate members. They were zealously guarded against the curiosity of outsiders. Emotions among Norsemen were not publicly shown. A stone face hid the heart's thoughts. It's a way to survive with honor. The Norseman's creed was that "real men" ought rather to die than cry. I've seen those faces.

CHAPTER 84

Chiefs, Earls And Kings
In The Viking World

S INCE THE DAWN OF THE human race, a few people have managed to become its leaders. In Oslo's Frogner Park, there is a famous monolith sculptured by Gustav Vigeland which portrays the mad race to the top of the heap. It reminds me of a game played in grade school called "the king of the hill." The challenge was to be on top and push all the others down.

We can only guess how chiefs, earls and kings came to be. My theory is that local chiefs have been around from the beginning through charisma, physical force or election. The early Vikings had their chiefs, but sometimes these called themselves "kings." In pagan times, dynastic kings made their claim to power as descendants of the gods. This was the case for the "Yngling" rulers of Norway to which the present royal family traces its roots. They came out second best in a power struggle in Sweden and moved to Norway. In Christian times, kings claimed to rule by "divine right."

No uniform rules were followed in all of the Scandinavian countries, but there are some basic patterns. The local chiefs were there first and coexisted with the coming of later royalty. There was tension between the "blue bloods" and those who rose up through local struggle. The foreign kings, conscious of their divine origins, felt that ruling was their right and that armed struggle for power over the local chiefs was justified. The families of royalty became a wealthy aristrocracy. Becoming wealthy was the "bottom line."

In Denmark, the local chief was called a "styraesman" (helmsman), a term used for a ship's captain. When they worked together, they had great power and even elected kings. In the assemblies of free men ("Things"), the leaders were called "hethwarthae maen" (men worthy of honor). They were called "lendsmen" (sheriffs or bailiffs) in Norway. I discovered that there was lendsman in my family tree about 400 years ago in western Norway. However, at that time they were the "king's men," and not chosen by the people. The stryraesman commanded a levy of 40 local men, a full ship's crew. The king's enforcers were called a "hird." It was expensive to maintain such a group and their dependants. Bishops also maintained hirds.

In Sweden, the king's farm was called "Husaby" (a house-village). It was run by the king's "bryti" (steward or bailiff). In Norway, the title "hersir" (landed man or "herr") was the equivalent to a baron in England. In Iceland, the local chief was called a "godi," a name strangely similar to "god." Iceland never had kings or national leaders. The godi was selected from families of distinction, likely from the earliest settlers (A.D. 870-930). All free men in Iceland were attached to a godi.

The "earls" (Jarls in Scandinavia) were among the country's most distinguished chiefs. Birger Jarl was one of Sweden's most famous rulers. King Harald Haarfagre appointed a jarl (earl) in each "fylke" (county) of Norway to insure his rule.

The title "king" ("konungr") means "a man of noted origin." Kings came from particular families and had to be elected by an assembly of free men with the title conferred in a recognized ceremony. An especially powerful king, however, might force a Thing (assembly) to elect him. The election involved an agreement by the king to provide military protection and sacrifices to the gods for a harvest, while the electors promised loyalty. Crop failures and economic depression were blamed on the king. If a series of droughts occurred, the king could be sacrificed to appease the gods. He was subject to the law and not above it.

Christianity greatly changed the idea of kingship. It claimed that the king's authority had to come from God as mediated by the church. A king could not rule without the approval of the church. This was in direct opposition to the earlier Scandinavian practice of election of kings by the chiefs and free men. It took about two centuries for the hierarchical practices of the church to overcome the ancient Viking customs.

In the Christian period, crimes against the land became acts against the king, as all the land was claimed by him. The Danes and Norwegians resisted these centralized encroachments against the authority of the local chiefs, but the power of the church prevailed. The kings had to enforce the tithe and see that Peter's pence was sent to Rome. The most successful kings were the great orators. They had no public address systems, so loud voices were an asset. Norway's most remembered kings, Olaf Tryggvason and Olaf Haraldsson, were "missionary Vikings" and ruled only a total of 20 years. Most kings did not live to become old. Few of them reached age 40. King Magnus is supposed to have said, "A king is for glory, not for long life."

The chiefs who rose up from the people were threatened by the kings who came from foreign lands with the claim that they had been born to rule. To this day, royalty remains a unique race of people who may not even have last names. I, however, come from the peasant stock of free men who gloried in being equals. My "republican" (Latin: "res publica") and "democratic" (Greek: "demos") prejudices have never felt the need for royalty as we knew them from the past. I've got too much of the old Norse love of freedom in my blood.

The present royal families of Denmark, Norway and Sweden, however, are a new kind of royalty whose commitment is to serve their countries. They are remarkable people and of great value to their nations. I'm proud to honor them for their dignity and noble services to the lands of my family's heritages.

CHAPTER 85

Everyday Life
In The Viking World

EVERYDAY LIFE MAY NOT MAKE prime TV, yet it is the stuff which produces good people. What was life really like in Viking days? We have two sources of information - archaeology and literature.

I have tried to form a mental picture of those days through the eyes of a child. My memory recalls early impressions of life in a Norwegian-American community. In some respects, it may have been closer to Viking days than the way I live now. One main difference is that I grew up in a house with floors, a chimney to let out the smoke and windows that opened.

Like the Viking world, most people in my home community lived on farms. Town people were mainly merchants, officials and skilled craftsmen in Viking times, and then only for part of the year. It was a big day when we hitched up the horses to a wagon or a sled (cars were used only in summer) and went to church or to town for shopping. I can still remember seeing neighbors driving to in a buggy to visit at our farm during the summertime.

The Norseman's first concern was survival. Starvation, cold and disease were a constant battle. Games and parties had to wait until the work was done. There was, of course, quite a difference between the warmer climates of Denmark and Iceland as opposed to Finland, Norway and Sweden. In those days, Denmark controlled much of southern Sweden. The Danes and Icelanders could afford some luxuries, but the other Scandinavians countries had a bleaker life.

Cereal grains were grown in the warmer climates. Animal husbandry was more important in the cold north. Rye, oats and barley, together with peas, cabbage, garlic, leek and wild berries were harvested. Even seaweed was used for food and fodder. But everywere in Scandinavia, hunting and fishing were a way of life. Reindeer, elk, bear, red deer and rabbits were part of the food supply, together with fish. Seals were also

189

hunted. There was famine when herring failed to return and crops did not grow.

We know more about the rich and the slaves than about the small land owner, for only the rich could afford to be buried in a Viking ship with all kinds of artifacts that have been preserved in the cold clay.

Lindholm Hoje in northern Denmark is the most carefully studied Viking village. I visited there and felt the ancient past while trudging over the surface. The shape of houses can be determined as well as the remains of a metalworking industry. The courtyard house is an example of their buildings. I've visited modern Danish farms that still have the same pattern. The family dwelling, granaries, workshop, mill and barn are joined in one large building. The Viking farm complex has even been found in the Shetland Islands. Sir Walter Scott romantically named one such place "Jarlshof."

Eating, sleeping and sitting were the most common activities provided for in the home. They also had chests for clothes, but closets and cupboards were unknown. The kitchen was the most important room. The food was either grown on the farm or bought at the local market. Only spices and wines were imported. Some wines may have been domestic. Dairy products were popular. Mead, an alcoholic drink, was made with a honey base. Beer was malted from barley and hops. The Vikings were men of great thirst and drinking was both a social and a religious obligation.

Two meals a day were served. Without refrigerators and microwaves, preparing two meals could take a great deal of time, not to mention all the other work that women had to do. The homes were generally untidy and unclean. This is one of the reasons that leprosy was such a problem in Norway. Windows, if any, were small and made of the glaze of a stomach membrane from a farm animal. Glass was too expensive. Shutters covered the membranes.

Children got a useful education in the home. Wool was sheared, cleaned, carded, spun and finally made into "wadmal," i.e. measured cloth. It was used for currency in Iceland. The farm on which I grew up also had the equipment to card wool and a spinning wheel so we could make our own wool cloth, besides repairing harnesses and shoes.

I can't remember ever seeing cloth made on our farm, however. The Old Norse farm was a self-contained unit, making almost everything it needed. This is quite a contrast to our modern ways of having to buy everything we need in modern shopping centers.

Unmarried girls wore their hair long with a band across the head, but married women put their hair up in a knot covered by a bonnet. Embroidery was a way a woman could distinguish herself and prove herself a better catch for marriage.

Plows were made mostly of wood, but people often tilled with a wooden spade. Metal workers made a good living, because they combined blacksmithing with making jewelry. One of the biggest tool chests has been found at Morgedal, Norway. It had everything needed for carpentry and metal work.

It's true that "all work and no play makes Ole a dull boy," but too much leisure corrupts good manners. Drunkenness, brawling and bloodshed became a way of life to Norsemen. The rich indulged more than the poor because they could afford it, but the poor tend to imitate the rich. Parties in the homes consisted of reciting poetry, asking riddles, telling stories and dancing. Games were invented with dice, checkers and chess. It's unfortunate that we hardly know anything about music in the old Norse times, though they had harps, fiddles and pipes.

Outdoor sports included feats of strength, archery, horse racing and horse fighting. But it was "never on Sunday!" The story is told that St. Olaf was once whittling, forgetting that it was the Lord's day. When reminded, he gathered the chips and burned them in the palm of his hand.

CHAPTER 86

Erling Rolfsrud And
the 'Tiger Lily Years'

I FIRST MET ERLING NIKOLAI ROLFSRUD in the fall of 1944 when I was a freshman at Concordia College in Moorhead, Minnesota. He was Chairman of the Department of Business Education and I was a half-scared boy that barely got off the tractor in time to start school. I never took any business classes from him, but I always felt that he liked me. This was reassuring to the country boy who was reared with immigrant values.

Rolfsrud left Concordia after that year and I can't remember meeting him again until the 1986 Norsk Høstfest. During these years, he became one of the best known writers in the Midwest. We read his books to our children. "Gopher Tails for Papa" (1951) and "Boy from Johnny Butte" (1956) were part of their growing up.

His book, "Scandinavian Moses" (1986) brought him to Minot for the Høstfest. It's the story of Knute Nelson, an immigrant boy from Norway, who was as important in politics to Norwegian Americans as Martin Luther King was to Black Americans. His success broke the barrier that had kept the Norsk immigrants in "bondage." From 1882 until his death in 1923, Nelson was a Congressman, Governor and Senator from Minnesota. Rolfsrud returned to the Høstfest in 1987 with "Notable North Dakotans," which includes several stories on Scandinavians.

Having done an article on Nelson in the "Scandinavian Heritage" column, I asked Rolfsrud how he happened to write a book about this "grand old man of Minnesota." I should have known. Rolfsrud's home is near Alexandria where Nelson had lived. He'd been involved in saving the Nelson house as an historical building.

Rolfsrud has written 26 books on a wide range of subjects since his "Lanterns Over the Prairies" in 1949. After the Høstfest, I called him and said I'd like to do a story on him. He kindly consented to share some anecdotal material. I especially asked for information about his boyhood. He sent me his book, "The Tiger-Lily Years" (1975), which was written for his children and grandchildren to tell them what life was like before "supersonic transportation, shopping malls, plastic flowers, and quick food stops." It describes his growing up on a farm near Keene, North Dakota, and attending a country grade school in the far western part of the state.

This man who has become one of the outstanding Midwest writers was sent out to pick tiger lilies for his father's funeral. The book is his "confession" about the meaning of life learned in the aftermath of those days. While his older brother Halvor took over the man's work on the farm at age 14, Erling discovered that he liked to do the things that were teasing material for other boys. He enjoyed flowers, playing the organ and books. Of course, he also liked it when Halvor let him drive the horses to town with a load of grain or the tractor for plowing. Halvor went on to be a successful farmer and a highly regarded state legislator. It was to his immigrant mother, however, that Rolfsrud pays the highest tributes. She inspired the desire in him for an education.

I always like to find out about the child that precedes the adult. Children are, I believe, the most exciting people in the world. Having read "The Tiger-Lily Years," I now understand why Erling Rolfsrud is still the delightful person I'd known him to be. He discovered that the Yankee neighbors hugged and kissed their children. In the Rolfsrud home, like in so many Norwegian homes, children were expected to know that their parents loved them without a display of affections. Affection would "spoil" them. Rolfsrud liked the Yankee ways better.

Rolfsrud's memory has phenomenal recall. He gives minute details about the cost of a mackinaw from Sears & Roebuck ($5.45), details on cars which the neighbors drove, the description of his new suit with longs pants for eighth grade graduation and gathering 17 sacks of cow chips as a birthday present for his mother.

Besides writing books, Rolfsrud also has a weekly syndicated column which appears in newspapers throughout North Dakota and Minnesota. As expected, they're excellently written and fascinating to read. He writes on a wide variety of subjects. The one which has interested me most was his reflections on "hardships" while a college student in the early 1930s. He relates how he taught in a one-room grade school in 1930 for $81 per month. To qualify for the job, he borrowed $120 from a bank to attend summer school at the Minot State Teacher's College. Staying in the schoolhouse, he walked 14 miles home for the weekends when his brother could not come and get him. After three years of teaching, despite reducing salaries due to the Depression, he saved enough to finance one year at Concordia College. He washed a lot of dishes for his college degree which was earned in three years.

All through his life, the church has been important to Rolfsrud. Besides writing articles for Sunday School papers, he has been a church organist for 30 years.

We compared some notes about writing and I was not surpised to learn that he has that inner compulsion of necessity which drives many of us to write. For two years, he was Associate Editor of "The North Dakota Teacher" and also lectured in 175 schools across the state. It was fitting that Erling Rolfsrud was selected as one of the 75 "heroes" of North Dakota in 1964 for the state's Diamond Jubilee. Those "Tiger-Lily Years" have blossomed. I hope he brings another new book to the Høstfest next year.

CHAPTER 87

Count Folke Bernadotte —
Sweden's Humanitarian Diplomat

S WEDEN HAS HAD MORE than its share of outstanding people. Up until the 19th century, many had been military figures, but during the past two centuries their contributions have largely been humanitarian. Among them, few will rank above Count Folke Bernadotte (1895-1948).

Bernadotte descended from Napoleon's Marshall, Jean Baptiste Jules Bernadotte, who became Sweden's Crown Prince when the Vasa family ran out of male heirs 175 years ago. The Count's great grandfather was a French nobleman who had hoped to become king of France after Napoleon's defeat. Sweden may have been his second choice, but he was a good choice for the Swedes. Taking the name Karl XIV Johan, he was king of both Sweden and Norway from 1818-1844.

Those of us who come from peasant background often have difficulty appreciating the valuable contributions of royal families. We're easily biased by our republican outlook on government. Count Folke Bernadotte is an example of a relative of the royal house of Sweden who took service to his nation and to the world seriously.

As Hitler's "Thousand Year Reich" was crumbling in early 1945, a fearful omen occured in Norway. Thirty-four patriots were executed in February. This was a sign of Nazi nervousness. Every effort had to be used to get the 15,000 Scandinavian prisoners out of the German concentration camps. Living conditions had been vile and the interned Scandinavians were in special danger. Intelligence learned that all prisoners were to be liquidated.

Bernadotte had already proven himself to be a skilled diplomat in Sweden. Now came the biggest challenge he had ever faced. At King Gustav's urging, he arranged a meeting with Heinrich Himmler, head of the feared SS troops, and argued that relations between Sweden and Germany needed improvement. As a token of good will, he presented the Reichsfuehrer with a book on Scandinavian runic inscriptions, a favorite study of the Nazi leader. Bernadotte proposed that the Scandinavian prisoners be allowed to return to their homelands. After some negotiating, Himmler agreed on condition that the Swedes would furnish the transportation. Thus began the famous convoys of white busses with red crosses painted on the roofs and sides. During April 1945, the busses ran continually. Once across the Danish border, they were greeted with food and flowers.

When the war ended, General Eisenhower invited Bernadotte to visit him in Paris. While there he convinced the future president, over Gen. Bedel-Smith's and Gen. Lucius Clay's objections, to allow the Swedish Red Cross to do relief work for German children under age 12. When the Russians, who were occupying northern Norway, ignored the needs of 100,000 starving Norwegians, Bernadotte went to them with aid. He also supplied 10,000 Soviet soldiers with new uniforms to wear as they were released from German prison camps in Norway. But it was in vain. When they arrived in their homeland, they were mowed down with machine gun fire for having been prisoners. Stalin did not dare to allow back into the country those who had seen the outside world.

Bernadotte's humanitarian work did not end with the white busses. He helped rescue 70,000 prisoners who were slaveworkers in the north of Norway. Besides directing the Swedish Red Cross to save Polish and German children, he brought aid to suffering areas of Finland, Hungary, Roumania and Greece. In 1946, he was named Chairman of the Swedish Red Cross. For this service, he never received a salary, only a token stipend. Fortunately, he was willing to use his own money for this humanitarian effort.

The great Swedish humanitarian was honored by many governments after the war. Poland awarded him the Order of the White Eagle, reserved for heads of State. No honors, however, came from the Soviet Union, which charged that the Swedish Red Cross was "Pro-Fascist."

In May 1948, Trygve Lie, the United Nations Secretary General, asked Bernadotte to go to Palestine. This was the year that the British Mandate ended and the State of Israel came into being. This resulted in thousands of Arab refugees. It was a time of bad tempers. Each side was convinced that it was right. Bernadotte, known for his openness to people of all religious creeds, was the right man for the job.

He produced the miracle that brought peace to the land. On June 11, 1948, a cease-fire was accepted by both sides. When asked how this happened, he said: "My father away back home is more than 80 years of age. When I came out here on this job, he gave me a new Bible. And he promised every day to remember me in his prayers. He is not alone. Thousands of Christians have promised to beseech God on my behalf. It is my conviction that without God's help and support this result would never have come about."

On September 17, 1948, 119 days after arriving in the troubled land, he was gunned down by soldiers while passing through Israeli territory at the foot of the "Hill of Evil," where legends say Jesus was tempted. I have been there. Being a "peacemaker" is a high risk profession, but I hope the world will always have such noble minded persons willing to take these risks. Long live the Bernadottes and their kind!

CHAPTER 88

Trade And Commerce
In The Viking World

WHEN THE NORSEMEN broke out from their isolation, they travelled with a crusader's passion. The first to leave went as pirates and raiders, but the bonafide traders were not far behind. It was important for people to know the difference, as a sheriff in England met his death thinking he was meeting traders when they were raiders.

We don't know much about the local commerce within the countries. It's safe to say, however, that barter was the earliest form of exchange. Not long after their "breakout," the Norse kings started to mint their own coins like they had seen in other parts of the world. Silver was the most common metal used for trade.

Furs were their most important export. The chief sources were Greenland, Finland, Lapland and even Newfoundland. Greenland also supplied ivory from walrus tusks, rope, hides and falcons. When the north German and Polish towns started to boom in the 12th century, there was an increased demand for food. This spurred the fishing industry of the Lofoten Islands and Iceland.

Market towns grew up in good harbors. The most famous of those in Denmark was Hedeby, near the German border in south Jutland. It started up about 800 A.D. and was destroyed with fire in 1050 by the Norwegian king, Harald Hardrada. Hebeby was an international trading center, located near the present city of Schleswig, with much of its business directed toward the German towns. Other Danish centers of trade were Aalborg, Aarhus, Ribe, Ringsted, Roskilde and Viborg. Aarhus, on the east coast of Jutland, was a major trading site doing business chiefly with Scandinavian countries.

The earliest of the known Swedish trade centers was at Helgo on Lake Malar near the present city of Lillon. It was started in the fifth century and disappeared in the eighth. Helgo was replaced by Birka on the island of Bjorko which became a famous international trading center.

198

A great deal has been learned of it through archaeological excavations from 1870 to 1885. I saw a display of artifacts from Birka at the Museum of Science and Industry in Chicago and was amazed at the ornate jewelry made of gold. Other places in Sweden known to have been trade centers were Lund, Sigtuna, Skara and Vastergarn. Lund became famous for its cathedral and university. As the home of an archbishop, it had considerable prestige.

Norway's most important early site was Kaupang, southwest of Oslo. It was a local market for the Scandinavian countries rather than an international center. Located near the earliest known settlements in the country, it's often mentioned in the sagas of Snorri Sturluson. Other important cities of Norway included Bergen, Oslo and Trondheim. Bergen became famous as the center of the Hanseatic League, a powerful alliance of north German merchants. Oslo, with its protected harbor, has ancient origins. The wooden buildings of Scandinavia were a fire hazard. When burned down, many cities came to a standstill unless rebuilt by foreign wealth.

The Norsemen also built towns in other lands. In Ireland, the Norwegians built Cork, Dublin, Limerick, Waterford and Wexford. There is some exciting excavation going on in Dublin today in search of the early Viking settlement. A small Celtic settlement existed there previously, but the Norsemen developed its harbor to winter their longships.

The most famous Norse site in England is York (Jorvik), once the center of Danish rule over the area called "Danelaw." The excavations have become a major attraction for tourists and students of history. Other places of Viking vintage in England include Derby, Leicester, Lincoln, Nottingham (home of "Robin Hood") and Stamford. The anthropological influence of the Danes and Norwegians on east England and the outer edges of Scotland is significant.

The Norse center in Normandy (northwest France) was Rouen. This was the place from which William the "Conqueror" hailed.

The Swedish Vikings made deep inroads into Russia beginning about 850 A.D. Many of their artifacts have been found at Kiev, the major city of early Russia, in a cemetery which covers 250 acres. It has over 4000 small mounds, many of which contain cremation urns. Soviet historians deny any real significance to the Viking presence in their land, even though the 12th century "Russian Primary Chronicle" claimed that the Norse presence was important to the development of Slavic nation-hood.

One of the national treasures of Czeckoslovakia is the "Sword of St. Stephen," kept in the cathedral at Prague. Scholars claim that this is a tenth century Viking weapon.

Besides cemeteries and the ruins of ancient cities, one of the most interesting finds has been buried coins. 10,000 coins left behind by Vikings have been found in Estonia. These were buried to keep them from falling into the hands of raiders. Latvia and Poland also have produced Viking artifacts.

As communities grew, the merchants formed guilds for protection and to stimulate the economy. They also controlled the knowledge of skills which they passed on within their own families and to favorites. They became masters in the art of bargaining, dealing in silk, wine and slaves, as well as furs and handcrafted articles. Viking swords were much in demand. The Norsemen had a sharp eye for business. Those of you who have visited their lands today know that they still have.

CHAPTER 89

Warfare In
The Viking World

WAR IS THE ULTIMATE CONTEST in the games people play. The Vikings were no exception. While they are mostly remembered for their sudden attacks upon unsuspecting communities, they also built defensive works.

The "Danevirke" was the Danish version of the Maginot and Siegfried Lines of modern times. It was a ditch with an earth embankment across the southern border of Jutland, built in 808 by the Danish King Godfred to defend Hedeby, Denmark's main trading center, against Emperor Charlemagne. Typical of the defenses built in England and in western Europe, it's the only major military mound surviving in Scandinavia today. The Danevirke, faced with timbers and crowned with a palisade, varied from 15 to 20 feet high.

The Vikings were primarily farmers and traders, but war necessarily loomed large in their lives. There were also professional soldiers. Men between the ages of 18 and 50 could volunteer to become a part of this warrior society. They lived under strict discipline of loyalty and vengeance. The booty was shared on their return from an expedition. No women were allowed in camp and three days was the maximum leave allowed at one time.

Several military camps can be identified in Denmark. They are located at Trelleborg in West Sjaeland (Zealand), Aggersborg on the Limfjord near Aalborg, Fyrkat near Hobro in East Jutland and at Nonnebakken in Odense on the island of Fyn. The barracks were encircled by a ditch with banks over 20 feet high and housed up to 50 men each. They were staging areas for the invasion of England by Kings Svein Forkbeard and Knut the Great. The Danes could afford the expense as they were collecting "Danegeld" (bribe money) from the French and the English to stay away. But they always returned when they ran short of cash. The outlines of these camps are clearly visible to aerial photography.

Every able-bodied adult man was required to maintain weapons in his home. Annual inspections were made to make sure that they were kept in good condition. The sword was the most important weapon, but spear, shield, helmet, mail-coat, axe and a bow with three dozen arrows made up a farmer's armory. Weapons were for protection in war and a mark of distinction during peace.

The wealthy spent great sums on decorations for their weapons, including gold and silver adornments. Weapons were also a good capital investment, just like gun collections today. It was common for swords to have a name engraved on the blade. Some swords were said to have magic in them and inspired fear in the enemy. Names like "Leg-biter," "Fierce," "Long-and-sharp," and "Gold-hilt" were used. Sword making was a carefully guarded skill and brought great profits to those whose reputations were established. Swords captured in battle became prized trophies displayed in homes. Many weapons of Viking times have been found.

If an attack was made on a district, every man, including slaves, was required to fight off the invaders. Kings had authority to impose a levy of ships, men, armaments and supplies. The Norsemen were especially skilled at sea battles. They lashed their ships together and fought as though on land. Banners were important to the morale of the warriors. As long as the standard-bearer did his job, the soldiers knew that their cause was alive.

Before battle, it was customary for the leader to make an oration to inspire courage. Sacrifices were made in heathen times to the gods for victory and a javelin was hurled into the air as a symbolic action to show that the enemy was doomed. In Christian times, war songs and chants were used. The song "Fram, fram, St. Olaf" ("Forward, forward, St. Olaf") is based on these war songs.

Horses were not used much in Viking wars. The Fjord-horses were raised for peace. But the Swedes and Danes did develop a cavalry in the 12th century.

There was not much of an "art" to warfare. The object was to bash the enemy to death. One of the strategies was not to fight with sun in the eyes. A wedge formation was a standard pattern of attack.

The "berserks" were a group of "crazies" wearing bearskin shirts who worked themselves into a frenzy and attacked with wild howling on a dead run. Their condition may have been induced by alcohol or drugs with the belief that they had the power of wild bears. Berserks were prized as warriors but otherwise considered stupid and demon possessed.

Churches were often places of sanctuary, though this was not always respected. "St. Knud," a Danish king, fled to the cathedral in Odense but was murdered on the spot by his enemies. I've visited the place.

There were no "peace movements" in those days. War was taken for granted and the "Just War," as defined by Christian theologians, was used to justify almost any kind of aggressive act. Peaceful arbitration was not an option in those days, like the separation of Norway and Sweden in 1905. Everything was settled by force.

Was the world safer then than now? Were those really the "good old days?" I am not sure that much has changed. Fear is still the most powerful dynamic in society. Human savagery is as much a part of life today as it was then. What has changed is the potential for mass killing which the ancients did not have. Only plagues, storms and volcanoes had such destructive power in those days and they were regarded as "acts of God," which seems unfair to God's "public relations," unless vengeance is his stock in trade.

CHAPTER 90

Christmas
In Scandinavia

SCANDINAVIANS LOVE SUMMER, but no season gives more excitement than Christmas. Christmas is celebrated mostly in the dark in the Nordic lands as the sun has gone south for the winter.

The Norsemen have kept careful watch for the return of the sun since earliest times. The ancient Norse kept a festival called "Jul" or "Yule," which came from "Joulu" (pronounced Yule-oo). It was a pagan festival all over northern Europe. Jul was a time of sacrifices to Norse gods in order to insure good crops for the following year. Huge amounts of ale were consumed during the holiday.

The Christian celebration of Christ's birth did not become popular in Rome until the fourth century. December 25 was picked as a challenge to the pagan worship of the sun. It was a time of drunkenness and debauchery. The earliest Christian celebration was Easter. The baptism of Jesus was celebrated on January 6 and has become the nativity celebration in Eastern Christianity. When "Christmas" was introduced into Jerusalem in 440, there were riots. That was before they realized its value for tourist promotion.

In Scandinavia the Christmas season begins on December 1. It's preceded by lots of preparations in the home. At least seven kinds of cookies are baked and house cleaning is thorough. Even the birds get special attention. Sheafs of grain are put on a pole. While visiting in Lyngdal (north of Kongsberg in Norway), I saw people preparing for the Christmas bird feeding as early as September. Cattle also get special attention since they had a part in the first Christmas.

Santa Claus has come to Scandinavia, but not the same "jolly old St. Nick" that we see in American department stores. In Finland, he is called "Joulupokki" and prefers to come on a bicycle to distribute gifts. In Sweden, he is called "Jultomen."

The "Julenissen" have a part in Christmas. The "nissen" were

204

friendly elves which lived on farms to bring good luck to the owners. The word seems to have derived from "Nicholas." On Christmas eve, the grateful farmers put out a bowl of cooked rice with milk in the barn for the nissen, otherwise he might move to another farm. It was also feared that he might even become angry and strangle a cow for revenge.

In Sweden, December 13 is a special day on the way to Christmas. It honors "St. Lucia," a young woman who became a Christian martyr in Sicily about 300. Irish missionaries brought the legend to Varmland and it is now a part of Swedish pre-Christmas celebrations everywhere, including America. It's a great honor for a Swedish girl to be chosen "Lucia." It's a festival occasion for the Swedish American Institute members in Minneapolis.

Scandinavians go to church at 4:00 p.m. on Christmas Eve. The lights, music and simple pageantry are deeply ingrained in their tradition. A "hush" falls over everyone as they enter the church.

After the services, they hurry home to eat. In many cases, this is the first time the children will have seen the Christmas tree. This tradition was also observed in America. As a child, I was never permitted to see the tree until Christmas Eve. Andreas Ueland wrote that the Christmas tree and gifts did not become a regular part of Norwegian Christmas celebrations until after 1800. Rice pudding is a favorite dish on that holy night. An almond is placed in one of the bowls. Whoever gets it is supposed to have "good luck" for the next year. It used to mean a happy marriage was in prospect for the singles in waiting.

The main Christmas dinner may still include lutefisk in Finland, Norway and Sweden. The Danes prefer roast goose and red cabbage, together with liver postej (liver paste), pumpernickel, klejner and tarts. They also put candles in their windows.

Music is important to a Scandinavian Christmas. They have given the world some beautiful songs. "Jeg er saa glad hver julekveld" ("I am so glad each Christmas Eve") from Norway combines both religious faith and culture. "Her kommer dine arme smaa" ("Thy little ones, dear Lord, are we") from the Danish tradition has a deep piety. A favorite song in Sweden is "Nar juldagsmorgon glimmar" ("When Christmas morn is dawning").

THE SCANDINAVIAN WORLD

Christmas is for children in Scandinavia, just like America. Danish children may be given a present each day, beginning December 1. On Christmas morning, they get their special gifts. In the olden days, Christmas lasted until Easter. Decorations were left up and the dark days of winter went faster.

"Annandag jul," the second day of Christmas, is used for visiting and giving presents. In my home community at Colfax, North Dakota, we'd have the Sunday School Christmas program on December 27. We didn't rush the celebrations to get them out of the way like it's done most places today. We'd often travel the five miles to town with horses and bobsled for our celebrations. No night in the year seemed to have such bright stars as that night and I'd keep looking for the star of Bethlehem to lead the way.

Charity for the poor was a part of a Scandinavian Christmas in past days, but under the present system of "Christian socialism," there are no poor today.

What I appreciate most about the Scandinavian Christmas customs is that families take time to be together as they celebrate. Materialism and commercialism threaten to crowd out the best of things for us. We start Christmas too early and put it out of our minds by December 26. The Scandinavians close up shop and enjoy their holidays in the privacy and enjoyment of their homes for a longer period of time. We'd do well to recover that part of the Scandinavian tradition.

CHAPTER 91

The Saga Of
Torger Skaaden

MOST OF THE RECORDS about immigrants to America have been lost forever. I know very little about the inner feelings and exact thoughts of my ancestors from Norway. They've not left so much as one written word for their families.

That makes the journalling of Torger Johannesen Skaaden significant. I was fortunate to examine a copy of his chronicle called "My Life's Adventure" or "Experiences in the School of Life." It was translated by Carl C. Damkaer of Upham, North Dakota, in 1920.

Skaaden was born November 28, 1836, in Norway, the son of Johan Skjonsberg and Ingeborg Skaal. He was the oldest of nine children. He wrote that his father was "not very religious," but his mother "more religious." She "taught us prayers and hymns which I will never forget."

His earliest memories were of a brother, Amund (who died at age five), a pair of sealskin pants and his first day at school. He remembered being told at bedtime to say prayers, cross himself three times and then "safely lie down and go to sleep."

Skaaden's early education consisted of lessons taught by an itinerant teacher who went from farm to farm, staying a week at each place. Among the documents which attracted him was the Norwegian constitution of 1814 from which he came to believe that the king in Stockholm was "holy."

He remembered his confirmation instruction from Pastor Nissen whom he called "an exceptionally good minister." He did not, however, get the religious "high" that he had expected from confirmation.

Today we plan our lives almost as if we were going to live forever. It was different in Torger Skaaden's world. Epidemics ravaged communities. There were many large families, but few who did not bury several children. It was common for a man to be married at least two or more times. Childbirth, hard work, unfriendly weather, lack of medical care and economic hardship separated many mothers from their families.

This also happened to Torger Skaaden. His first wife, Karen, journeyed with him to America and died within a year of arrival. Ingeborg, a ten-year-old daughter, became mother and housekeeper for the family which included a six-month-old child. Their first home in America, a 12 by 12 cabin with a dirt floor, did not offer many luxuries. Then Torger married Lisbet. Sixteen years later (1903), she also died. By this time they had homesteaded in McHenry County of North Dakota, having first settled in the Goose River Valley in eastern part of the state.

In 1906, at age 68, Torger returned to Norway to visit his family and friends. To his regret, most of them were no longer alive or still in the old home community. He had returned too late.

His journals told of crop failure which drove him to consult a Swedish pastor named Frantsen who advised him to tithe from his income. One night by candlelight, he read of a family in Minnesota whose house had burned down. They had lost everything. He was so moved that the next morning he got on his pony and collected 85 dollars for the unfortunate people. He observed that "the one who has the hardest time is the most willing to give."

World War I weighed heavily on the minds of the immigrant families. Like so many people, he was fascinated by the Book of Revelation, finding parallels in its descriptions to the early 20th century.

Death was an ever present shadow on the immigrant communities. He wrote: "I have seen death come in many different ways - at times quietly and peacefully, at other times with great struggle as when it came to our Master on the cross and he called out, 'My God, my God, why hast thou forsaken me?' " His early childhood training in the Bible comes through over and over again in these writings.

The story of Skaaden's struggles were not only concerned with economics, diseases and death. It was also the inner struggle of faith against the fatalism that comes from contemplating the sovereignty of God. Torger could resign himself to God's ultimate authority, but yet he struggled with the issues of life.

Like so many immigrants from Norway, his political convictions were to the "left." "Populism" was popular among these folks whose sense of nationalism in their homelands was strong. Constitutionally guaranteed freedoms and the right of self-determination burned in the hearts of these newcomers to America.

Skaaden's journal is no literary masterpiece, even though it shows a sensitive appreciation for good literature and poetry. There is much left out that the reader would like to have known about dates and places. The significant thing is that he wrote these journals at all. One wonders what he might have done with a college education. I think he might have gone far. He had a sense of vision to life and reflected meaningfully on his experiences. His family is richer for these memoirs. These writings are not the rambling thoughts of a barbarian, but of a man with a highly cultured soul. I wonder how many more of these prairie prophets have passed our way unnoticed.

CHAPTER 92

George Reishus
Remembers

THERE IS NOTHING SO EXCITING as seeing the world through the eyes of a child. One of the great losses to the world is that so much history is written by people who have forgotten their childhood perspectives. This was not the case with George Alfred Reishus (1886-1972), whose Norwegian family moved from Minnesota to Minot, North Dakota, in 1887 when the "Magic City" was just beginning. It was cowboy country in those days and Reishus has left us a vivid description of it in his book "Gone Are the Days," published in 1954.

The Reishus family was among the earliest of Norwegian families to settle in the Midwest. George's uncle, Torjus, who came to Minot in 1886 to become pastor of First Lutheran Church, was born at Koshkonong, Wisconsin, in 1847. This is one of the historic Norse settlements in America. George was an uncle to my long time friend, Dr. Roy Harrisville, professor at Luther Northwestern Theological Seminary in St. Paul, Minnesota. So I find his recollections doubly interesting.

His early remembrance of Minot was as a city of cowboys, gunslingers, Indians, hunters, trappers, gamblers, construction crews, fistfights, scouts, "fancy girls," merchants and farmers. He recalled that there were were two places he was forbidden to go near. One was the row of houses near the railroad tracks where the "fancy girls" lived with their red lamps burning night and day. The other was the coulees in the southwest part of the town because the Indians encamped on what we now know as "South Hill," where I've lived for 14 years. He told the story how his new cap was swished from his head one day when he ventured too close to the forbidden coulees. It took a trip with his father to the teepees to recover it.

He remembered the courage of the frontier women. His own mother, Astrid, known for her gentleness, took off with a butcher knife one day when two strolling squaws snatched some loaves of bread cooling in

210

her window. The loaves were recovered. It could be dangerous for a woman to be home alone when her husband was seen leaving the farm. One brave woman carried on a conversation with an imaginary man, supposedly cleaning his rifle, until the eavesdropping marauders were frightened away.

Worst of all were the winters. Those three day blizzards, followed by intense cold, were death to travellers and to homes caught without their supply of firewood hauled from the river. (I remember that my father went to the Wild Rice River to bring home wood for burning every year.) In such storms, the oxen were the surest guides to find the way home through the blinding snow. Reishus told the story about when his sister became severely ill and the doctor in Minot was not available. Oxen were dispatched during a storm with a message tied to their horns to Uncle Torjus, the pastor, to come. He came to pray before she died.

Like all boys (and I was no exception), he admired cowboys. One of his most interesting stories was when three unbranded calves were missing from the farm. They had strayed off to a large cattle ranch just in time for the branding party. Young George decided that this was his opportunity to get to know some real cowboys and have some man-talk with them. While there, he decided to see if the missing calves were in the herd. But how could he tell? This would seem to be an impossible task, but not for George. He called out in Norwegian, "Kom Kjyra, Kom Kjyra," from the song "Seterjenten Sondag" (the "Chalet Girl's Sunday"), made popular by the famous Jenny Lind, the "Swedish Nightingale." Sure enough, three calves came bounding out and were released to him by the ranchers, despite their new brands. The calves understood Norwegian!

Education was irregular but critical to the pioneers. They realized that their lack of education was a great handicap. A group of 20 farmers organized in the winter of 1898 to start a school for themselves and hired George's father, Gunder, to be their teacher. They paid him $40 a month and helped with his chores on Saturdays. English was the top priority and "King's English" at that. History and citizenship also received top billing.

He told of waiting for hunting season at age 10. All summer long he had watched and protected a covey of prairie chickens. But when the season opened, he had to shock grain. In desperation, he smuggled a shotgun and some shells into the field. Then he saw a buckboard coming with some hunters directly to his protected game. George met the invaders, took bead on one of their dogs and promised to blow its head off if they went after his chickens. They backed off after calling him some abusive names, including "a white-haired Swede." That was a nasty lie! He didn't have white hair and he was 100% Norwegian! George got his revenge years later when he cast the deciding vote against the man who maligned him at the election for the presidency of an oil company. There is a moral to this story. Treat children with respect. They could grow up to be your best friends. I count many of them as mine.

George grew up to be city auditor, a state legislator and active in selling insurance, machinery and clothing. His recollections are cleverly written with a good dose of humor. I wish I had known him.

CHAPTER 93

Vikings In The
Turtle Mountains?

I F ANYONE SHOULD SERIOUSLY suggest that Norsemen once set up camp in North Dakota's Turtle Mountains, the anticipated response would be, "You got to be kidding!" But before you draw your final conclusions, you should read what John Molberg has written in his little book, "Vikings!"

I'd heard about his discoveries a few years ago and had wanted to learn more about them. Molberg sent me a copy of his book and I found it interesting. I'm not an authority on geology and archaeology, but I've read too much about the Norsemen to hastily doubt their abilities.

What is it that Molberg claimed might have been? Simply this, that 14th century Norsemen may have brought their boats to the Turtle Mountains on the North Dakota/Manitoba border. What evidence did he offer? Some granite boulders. Not just ordinary rocks, but rocks with holes cut into them. He concluded that the holes were not made by nature, but by man. He also believed that the boulders, which weighed several tons, were not hauled in from some other place, nor did an early settler drill the holes with the idea of blasting them with dynamite. Since the slopes were too steep for farming, he doesn't think that the rocks were dug up to clear land.

For what were these rocks used then? Molberg suggested that they might have been mooring stones into which the Norsemen put a pin to anchor their boats. Altogether, five such stones were found in the area. That would have required the water level from the Glacial Lake Souris to have covered the present site of Bottineau and lapped right up into the foothills of the Turtle Mountains. The boulders were at approximately the same elevation, about 2000 feet. The book has photographs of the boulders.

Equally fascinating are photos of a stone arched cave in the western foothills of the Turtle Mountains. No mortar had been used to hold the stones in place. Near the cave was the stone foundation of a building

213

that had once stood there. The cave is 8 feet wide, 13 feet long and 4 1/2 feet high. Since the rear of the cave had fallen in, it must have been much larger at one time. Could this have been a Viking shelter?

Besides the unusual rocks, a Roman sword had been found at the eastern edge of the Turtle Mountains at St. John, North Dakota, in the late 1960s. An axe head was found a couple of miles across the border into Canada. It bears the shape of a Viking battle axe. A chisel was also found. As if that were not enough, he also notes that some grave sites were found in the area originally thought to be Indian graves. Prof. Edward Milligan, a recognized authority on Native American culture, found them different from any he had seen.

Mooring stones have been found in many places like those believed to have been used by Norsemen for anchoring their ships. Molberg made some serious attempts to check out his theory on these boulders. He consulted the faculty at the North Dakota State University in Bottineau to offer their critique. He's done his homework on Norse history too.

Molberg's findings and theories are by no means an open and shut case. Few things are in these matters. One of the problems is the 500 foot differential in elevation between the Glacial Lake Souris level and the level of the spillway into the Sheyenne River. He has an explanation for this too. Based on Charles Hapgood's theory of a shift in the earth's crust, is it possible that this has caused a change in the elevation of the Turtle Mountains in the last 600 years? We know that the earth is not a solid mass, as was supposed a few hundred years ago. It's a turbulent planet, full of life. The ocean floors are constantly shifting and earthquakes occuring.

How might the Norsemen have travelled to the Turtle Mountains? Molberg suggested that they came across the Atlantic (perhaps from Iceland) into the St. Lawrence River to the Great Lakes, the Chicago River, the Mississippi River, the Minnesota River, Lake Traverse, Lake Agassiz, the Sheyenne River and into Lake Souris. Or might they have travelled from Hudson Bay via the Souris River to these mooring points?

Molberg asked what happened to Vikings who may have come to the Turtle Mountains before Columbus's time. Obviously, they moved on.

To where? Well, he wondered if they were the reason why some Mandan Indians had "blue eyes and a fair complexion." While perhaps an overworked theory, it sounds as good as some of the other ideas I've heard.

What can we say about these discoveries? Tempting as it might be to declare these theories facts, we cannot and Molberg didn't. But together with the vast amount of data popping up all over the New World, it certainly suggests that many feet have stepped across this land before we arrived. Perhaps some day we'll have more evidence. But there's a problem with archaeological and geological finds. How should we interpret them? There is no printed manuscript accompanying them. And if there was, it surely would evoke disagreement, like the Kensington Stone. Unfortunately, Molberg died at the time I wrote my original story on his findings, so he never had a chance to read my article. I was hoping to visit with him about it.

Lloyd Heuesers, a science teacher at Central High School in Minot, read my article with interest and gave me some maps of the glacial Lake Souris which I had not previously seen. They make Molberg's hypothesis seem even more interesting.

In a time when we have such excellent possibilities for sharing knowledge, I have hopes that we will get reasonable answers to many of our questions. Molberg wrote: "Naturally, one would like to get definite proof; we will keep looking for a 14th century sign saying, 'Ole vas here.'"

CHAPTER 94

The Enigma Of
Vikdun Quisling

THERE ARE MANY WAYS to fame and remembrance, but few of us would like our name to be in the dictionaries as a byword. Vikdun Abraham Lauritz Jonsson Quisling (1887-1945) has that distinction. The Merriam-Webster Dictionary refers to his name as someone who betrays his country and collaborates with the enemy.

Who was this man whose name is remembered with infamy by the whole world? It's not any easy story for a person of Norwegian heritage to tell. Vikdun Quisling was born in Fyresdal, Telemark, where his ancestors had provided the pastors for generations. They were also independent farmers and soldiers. His father, the rural dean of Lutheran clergy, was an eccentric intellectual, according to Paul M. Hayes, author of "Quisling: The Career and Political Ideas of Vikdun Quisling" (Indiana University Press, 1972). His mother also came from distinguished stock.

When Vikdun was 13, his father became pastor of the Gjerpen parish, near Skien. He had a brilliant academic record at the Skien high school, surpassing Henrik Ibsen, a distant relative. In 1905, he entered the Norwegian Military Academy and graduated with the highest records in the school's history. It was expected that he would have become either a pastor or a scientist. A bright future seemed assured.

Quisling, an apt student of languages, went to Russia, where Leon Trotsky offered to make him chief of staff in the Red Army in its war against the "Whites." He had also been invited to be an instructor for the Imperial Chinese Army. While turning down the Russian offer, he did spend many years there and became enamored of Communist ideology. Stalin's oppressive agricultural policies, however, changed his mind and he later became a bitter foe of Communism.

A fervent nationalist, Quisling's ambition was to be Norway's "savior" in a world that was becoming threatened with Communism and war.

This led him, as a disillusioned idealist, into the Nazi camp. Because of his aggressive and argumentative behavior, he alienated most of the people who might have helped him rise to prominence. In 1933, he organized the "Nasjonal Samling" ("National Unity") Party. Rejected at the polls, he started to negotiate with Hitler's aides and actually saw Der Fuehrer in Berlin on December 13, 1939. He urged a German invasion of Norway. His antagonists claim he was hoping to become the head of government in Oslo.

On April 9, 1940, "Operation Wilfed" was launched by the Nazis and Norway was occupied, but not without a struggle. The Nazis, however, didn't trust him or believe that he had a following among the people. It was assumed because of the neutralist position of the Norwegian government that the people would give no opposition. Even though they had not had a war for 116 years, nothing of the kind happened.

The war years were turbulent for Quisling and he made many trips to Germany to convince Hitler that he was their best bet for running the government. For the most part, he succeeded because the Nazi administration was so clumsy. In the early days of the invasion, Quisling made the Hotel Continental his headquarters. It's still an elegant hotel with excellent food service. I've stayed there a number of times. An attentive waitress "picked up" the list of cabinet members he was proposing and gave it to the Resistance. They went public with it. As a result, few were willing to accept the positions offered.

Still, Quisling succeeded in getting a large number of people to become dues paying members of his party. I've heard different figures ranging all the way from 40,000 to 70,000 and even more. His anti-Communist appeal lured many patriotic Norwegians to the Russian Front. A friend told me that her father volunteered so that his children "would not have to fight the Communists in Norway." After the war, her father was fined heavily and served a jail sentence. Knut Hamsun, the great novelist, also became an ardent National Unity Party member.

When the war ended on May 9, 1945, Quisling went to the Police Station to negotiate a truce with the Resistance leaders. He was promptly arrested. After a highly publicized trial, he was found "guilty" and sentenced to death by a judge who had spent much of the war in a concentration camp. Quisling was executed at Akershus Castle about

2:30 a.m. on October 24, 1945. A gallery of distinguished sightseers was on hand to watch.

There is a bit of irony to his trial. Norway did not have a death penalty before the Nazi invasion. Quisling summed up the verdict himself when he said, "This case . . . is not just another judicial matter, but a question of politics." He was sentenced under a military law of 1902. His last days were spent reading the Bible and his father's writings, but he never "repented." Before his execution, he shook hands with the members of the firing squad. He is buried in the Gjerpen cemetery.

It's a mystery how this promising student should have chosen such a destructive way of life. I believe there are several reasons. Quisling took himself too seriously and felt that because of his superior intellect he alone was qualified to govern Norway. He also had come to love nature but distrust people. Imagine what he might have become if he would have had a sense of humor about himself.

CHAPTER 95

When The Vikings
Came To Troyes

I T ALWAYS SURPRISES ME how much travelling is done in our world. "Tourism" is by no means a recent innovation. It's been around for a long time. Adventure, curiosity, conquest and trade have made travellers out of the human race.

The Vikings were especially good at getting around. Among the places that they discovered was Troyes, a city of 10,000, on the main trade route to the southeast of Paris. After the Roman Empire collapsed, peace was always threatened and walls had to be built around the major cities. "Sacking" was what everyone had to get used to in those days. It must have been frightfully discouraging.

Joseph and Frances Gies in their book "Life in a Medieval City" state, "The champion raiders, who appeared late in the ninth century, were the Vikings." They referred to the Norsemen as "these red-bearded roughnecks from the far north." It's true that they had taken apart nearly every town on the map. In the province of Champagne, a local opportunist named Hastings joined them and returned to Norway. Then he led a series of raids into northwestern France.

The Vikings also contributed to the local economy because they'd sell their surplus plunder to towns that were strong enough to resist their attacks. Dublin in Ireland and York in England became trading posts to sell their stolen goods. When the walls were built well enough, the Norsemen were repelled as they did not bring battering rams and seige instruments. While they were still pagans, nothing was sacred. In fact Christians were a special object of their attacks. The cathedral of St. Pierre (Peter) and St. Paul in Troyes was burned to the ground in 891, just 14 years after Pope John VIII (872-882) held a council in it.

What was the attraction of Troyes? It hosted one of the biggest trade fairs in Europe during the Middle Ages. Held in July and August, it was called the "Hot Fair." The "Cold Fair" was held in November and December. Besides the fair at Troyes, there were four other fairs in the province of Champagne.

These fairs were important to the local economy as well as trade for a large area. Hanse merchants came from Germany, Italians crossed the snow-covered Alps, cloth caravans drove from Flanders, besides merchants from Spain and the Middle East. The Vikings didn't have wheeled plows, iron harrows, felling axes, horse collars or horse shoes, besides many other new inventions on display and for sale. The Scandinavians brought gold, silver and furs for trade in Troyes. When the "Viking" era ended after 1066, Scandinavians continued to travel to Troyes for the fairs.

Getting ready for the trade fair was important to these cities for another reason. It meant a careful clean-up of the city. The streets were narrow and there was no adequate sewage and garbage disposal or fire protection. Cleaning, however, did not remove the unpleasant odors that were a permanent part of the city. Diseases and epidemics were always a threat. Animal dung, the fish market, linen makers and worst of all was the smell coming from the butchers and tanners. When it rained, the streets became soggy with mud. Dogs, cats and pigeons were everywhere foraging for food.

The Scandinavians who came to Troyes had spices on their shopping list. These were popular items for trade in their own country. Saffron was worth more than its weight in gold. Cinnamon, nutmeg, and ginger were brought in from the Far East and claimed a dear price. Pepper was also a costly item and was used for flavoring and preserving meat. "Dear as pepper" was a common saying. Single peppercorns were even sold to housewives.

Merchants bringing caravans of goods were protected by the laws and treaties between countries and cities. A ruler would have to make good any losses which traders suffered from bandits while travelling to the trade fair in the borders of his country. Failure to honor such commitments might mean that a fair was either boycotted or that goods from another place were banned.

Troyes was a city of churches. Their bells began ringing at daybreak and were rung every three hours. This is how people could tell time as the weight-driven clock was not invented until the later Middle Ages. They had a saying, "Where are you from? I'm from Troyes. What do you do there? We ring."

Churches were used for more than prayer and the shrines of saints. Religious plays turned the churches into theatres. Biblical stories on Adam and Eve, Cain and Able, the prophets and the Easter story were popular. Since the church was usually the largest building in a village or city, it was also used for secular purposes, including the meetings of the town councils and trade guilds.

The visitors from far north Scandinavia would get quite an experience from this city of France. When they returned home with their purchases for resale in their marketplaces, visitors would come and stare, and some would buy. But equally interesting and welcome was the storyteller who had been to such distant places and told the people back home about the wonders of foreign travel. Such an art could keep a person with bed and board for many months during the long winters. Their stories became the inspiration for children to dream about the day that they'd be able to see these wonders for themselves. Many did.

CHAPTER 96

'Gamle Norge — Old Norway'

"KAN DU GLEMME GAMLE NORGE?" ("Can you forget old Norway?") This song is still sung by the children of immigrants who have never seen the shores of that far north land. But what was "old Norway" like? Jon Leirfall, from Stjordalen in the Trondheim area, has written an excellent book entitled "Old Times in Norway." It's one of the most helpful books I've read to understand the Norway which shaped the lives of the immigrant period (1825-1925).

Leirfall, born in 1899, is famous in Norway both as a writer and a politician. He was a prominent leader in the Farmer's Party (Bondepartiet) and was a member of the Parliament from 1945 to 1969. He is a "grass roots" historian with a good sense of humor. He is also an honorary citizen of Minneapolis. Leirfall attended the 1986 Norsk Høstfest and was introduced as a relative of Myron Floren. I found him to be a delightful gentleman.

According to Leirfall, the new Norway began to emerge about 1840, although it took several generations before the change was complete. I suspect that traces of "old Norway" are as likely to be found in some parts of America as in Norway today. Reading his book helped me to understand my own past. There are some things that I had supposed were the peculiarities of the immigrants which really are rooted in a thousand or more years of culture. It was only in America that they stood out as "different."

Leirfall explains the terminology needed to understand life in the old country. Such terms as "bygd" (rural community), "gaard" (farm), "grend" (neighborhood), "Opphavsgaard" (the original farm site) and "smaabruk" (cotter's farm) are explained with examples. He tells what it was like to be a child growing up in those days when education, though limited, was highly honored, making the Norwegian immigrants some of the most literate newcomers to America. That's why they rose

222

quickly to positions of leadership, especially in politics.

In the age before instant communications, evenings were spent around the fireplace telling and re-telling the stories that were part of the community. The parafin lamp and the kitchen stove greatly altered this pattern.

I enjoyed his description of the cotter's life. These were the small farmers on the edge of the main farm. Since the big farm went by law to the oldest son (for which he was bound to care for his parents as long as they lived), younger sons had to move out. Many of them cleared patches of ground on the mountain sides and eked out a living by their tiny cottages. The cotter also had to work for the "bonder" (the boss farmer) to pay rent. When the emigration to northern Norway and America took place, thousands of these cottages became vacant and farm workers became scarce.

It was not long before letters from America arrived about the wonders of the New World with its opportunities and freedom. When some of the successful emigrants began to return, usually at Christmas time, they were honored almost as royalty. All their past sins and foolishness for leaving Norway were forgiven.

During the 19th century, after Norway came under the rule of the Swedish king, a spirit of nationalism arose. The constitution of 1814 inspired the drive to have a completely free nation to choose its own destiny. With the overload of population going mostly to America (800,000 out of a population of 1,700,000 in 1865), poverty decreased and the rights of the common man were asserted. The cotters (just the men) were given the right to vote in 1884 and universal manhood suffrage was granted in 1897. Norway was second only to Finland in giving women the right to vote.

During the Danish period (1380-1814) when Norway was ruled from Copenhagen, the written language took on a great deal of Danish spelling. During the Swedish Period (1814-1905), Norwegians started to return to the "Old Norse." For example, "Hagen" was restored to "Haakon," especially in respect to their new king, Haakon VII (1905-1958). "Dahl" (valley) returned to "dal." My maternal grandmother's name was Beret. I wondered why her mother and grandmother, besides two sisters had this name. Leirfall explains that custom dictated the names of both sons and daughters. My mother's name Anne, as well as Jorun, has occurred for many generations in our family. The name Anne (pronounced "Anneh") is carried through to one of our granddaughters. That's a good Norwegian custom.

The big event of the community was a wedding. In the old days, the party could last for a whole week. Among my Halling ancestors, this could be a frightning time. The "kniv-Hallings" wore knives and fighting often erupted when too much liquor was served at these drawn out celebrations. In anticipation of this, many wives packed their husband's burial clothes when they went to a "bryllup" (wedding). The morning after the ceremony, they were all served "Rommegrot" (cream porridge) for breakfast. This continues to be a delicacy among many children of immigrants.

The old ways have passed. And it's a good thing, too, because they were filled with unnecessary taboos and fears. Infant mortality was high, so was death through childbirth. Medical understanding was extremely limited. Still, those days continue to beckon with nostalgia and we continue to sing, "Kan du glemme gamle Norge?" Leirfall helps us not to forget.

Anne Marie Gaylor in her Bunad.

Who Are The
'Sons Of Norway?'

T HE WINTER OF 1894-1895 was bleak in Minneapolis. It was a time of depression, unemployment and poverty. The Norwegians of North Minneapolis started to talk about what they could do to help their families and neighbors in the event of illness and death. Most of them had come from the areas of Trondheim and Selbu in Tronderlag. They met in Ingebret Rognaas' hardware store because, at age 40, he was more experienced than the other newcomers, having lived in America for 26 years. He was from Valdres.

They exchanged a lot of ideas and held an organizational meeting on January 16, 1895. At first they planned to call it the "Bjornstjerne Bjornson Lodge," after the famous Norwegian writer. Deciding that this name was too dificult to say in English, they chose "Sonner af Norge" ("Sons of Norway"). All meetings were conducted in the Norwegian language. They voted in 1938 to change the official language of the organization to English and its monthly magazine changed in 1942. In 1896, they agreed to pay five dollars a week sick benefit to members and increased the funeral benefit to one hundred dollars.

We're indebted to Dr. Sverre Norborg, a native of Oslo, who has written a history of the Sons of Norway entitled "An American Saga." He had been a professor at the University of Minnesota, Augsburg and Macalaster Colleges, as well as pastor in the Bergen Cathedral, Norwegian Seaman's Church in Brooklyn and of the Norwegian Memorial Church in Chicago (Logan Square).

The Sons of Norway was organized "To unite in a fraternal organization men and women of Norwegian birth, descent or affiliation, who are of good moral character." The term "affiliation" opens membership to anyone who happens to like a Norwegian.

Sons of Norway lodges are found in 29 states plus three Canadian provinces and even in Norway. The 110,000 members are divided into eight districts. Seven are in the United States and Canada and District

Eight is in Norway. North Dakota and Montana, plus Alberta and Saskatchewan comprise District 4. The International Headquarters are at 1455 West Lake Street, Minneapolis, MN 55408.

The "Viking" magazine published by the Sons of Norway always has a cover picture of Norway. The January 1987 issue had stories about the Leif Erikson Lodge in Ballard, Washington, about Bjorn Lasserud (a great skier), a story about the "Lyngen Horse," plus stories about food and news from the eight districts. After reading it for a while, one gets the feeling of knowing all these Norwegians. Many non-Norwegians join the organization (and hold offices too).

I joined the Sons of Norway in 1975, when planning our first trip to Norway. As you would expect, it's a group which is highly prejudiced about the goodness and importance of Norway. But it's also an open group, without prejudice towards other ethnic groups. They've gotten over the feelings of rivalry with Sweden. These were strong in 1905 when Norway separated from its sister nation and got its own royal family.

Travel and trade between the United States and Norway is important to this organization. The "Viking" magazine has advertisements for clogs and boots, heritage books, travel to Scandinavia, bunads, language study, festivals in Norway, auto rentals in Norway, dishes with rosemaling designs, a youth camp in Norway, art work and insurance, just to mention a few things. Sons of Norway members may visit Norway often, but there is no doubt about their loyalty to the New World. Patriotism has always been a part of their character.

Some people have wondered about the use of the word "lodge" in the organization, as it sometimes raises issues of conflict about religion. Theodore Graebner, writing in "A Handbook of Organizations" (Concordia Publishing House, 1948), stated that the Sons of Norway is not a secret society and has no altar, prayers or funeral ceremonies. He noted that political or religious issues are not allowed at meetings and that the "objects of the order are the preservation of Norwegian culture in America." He regarded it as a "nationalist society" and offered no objections to it.

One of the special projects promoted by Sons of Norway is "Ski For

Light," a program which teaches blind people to ski. They also underwrote a project for college students to travel across Greenland one summer. This had never been done before. Brave kids! It wasn't easy. Their latest big promotion is the "USA Cup," an annual soccer tournament at Blaine, Minnesota (the Twin Cities area). More than 400 young Norwegians attend the event, as well as youth from all over the United States and other foreign countries. Modelled after the Norway Cup in Oslo, it's the largest youth soccer tournament in America.

I was present at the dedication of "Skogfjorden," the Concordia College Norwegian Language Camp near Bemidji, MN, over 20 years ago. The Sons of Norway was a major contributor to building this site. Our daughter, Lisa, and sons, John and Christopher, have attended the camp.

In June 1925, the Sons of Norway were involved in the Norse-American Centennial held at the Minnesota State Fair Grounds. Over 70,000 people were on hand as President Calvin Coolidge paid tribute to the Norwegian contributions to the United States. He said: "You have given your pledge to the Land of the Free. The pledge of the Norwegian people has never yet gone unredeemed." May it ever be so. We've come a long way since that cold day of January 1895 in our determination to be "united and true until Dovre falls" (a statement from the Constitution of 1814). The Dovre Mountains still stand.

Sons of Norway shield.

CHAPTER 98

The 'Bygdelag'
Movement In America

MORE THAN ANY PEOPLE I KNOW, the Norwegians loved to start ethnic organizations. In his book "A Folk Epic: The Bygdelag in America," Prof. Odd Lovoll of St. Olaf College, lists 129 "bygdelags" (community lodges). Almost every section of Norway was organized in America according to their communities in the homeland.

I hold membership in the "Hallinglaget" which was organized at Walcott, North Dakota, on March 9, 1907. I was reared on a farm just seven miles south of Walcott. Their first "stevne" (convention) was held on May 17 of that year. Halling is my oldest heritage in America, dating from Hemsedal in 1867. My other heritages are from Numedal, Romsdal and Tronderlag. They also have organizations. My parents, however, did not join the local Hallinglag. I think that the reason is that the Hallings used to have dances and played cards. The piety of our home overruled such things. My home was also one of total abstinence from alcohol, tobacco, profanity and field work on Sundays. Good Friday was also kept as a day of rest and worship. I've never regretted this lifestyle.

The Hallings, like other clans of Norwegians, were organized in several local branches besides their national organization. The people of Gudbrandsdal had six "lags," one of which was organized in Minot, ND, in 1930. Christian E. Lee was secretary of the Northwest Gudbrandsdalslag from 1938-1957. There were 15 Tronderlags. The Northwest Valdreslag was organized in Minot in 1930. North Dakota Governor R. A. Nestos was president of the Vosselaget in 1924-1925.

As was typical of the "lag" minded Norwegians, they organized a national "Council of Bygdelags" in 1916. They were a powerful social force among the immigrants and their families. It's estimated that 75,000 people were involved in these organizations by the 1920s. In those early days, the bygdelags and the Sons of Norway were often rivals and even in opposition to each other. The one thing they all agreed with was the "Syttende Mai" (17th of May), the celebration of Norway's Constitution of 1814. There was a great of emotion and sentiment in the drive to start these "lags."

Most of these immigrants came from the rural areas of Norway. These new associations in America helped them to remember who they were and gave them courage to survive. The bygdelag provided "community" to these otherwise often shy newcomers. But in their "clan" meetings, these immigrants took courage in the new land. Many people planned for months to attend the next annual convention. They kept the old traditions alive. Songs, dances, fiddle playing, religious customs, dress styles and food have been preserved through these associations. The Norsk Høstfest is a social event that has brought Sons of Norway and bygdelag members together in one large celebration. A look at the variety of bunads (national dress costumes) at the Høstfest shows that the customs are still alive. And they still meet.

These rural folks represented the romantic aspirations of Norwegian ideals, as uninfluenced by life in the big cities and by the Danish rule from 1380 to 1814. With it was a return to the older way of speaking. This revival was called "Landsmaal" (the language of the land). One observer stated that "Norway is a country of many nations which naturally draw together when they get outside the country."

Even though the bygdelags grew up in the cities, it was mostly rural people who were their organizers. They'd advertise their meetings in the newspapers. People never seemed to grow weary of listening to speeches and the music of their homelands. It was an exercise in nostalgia of which they never tired. I suspect that some of those speeches got to be dull and drawn out, but it was the language and dialect of "home" and this was the most comforting sound that could come to their ears. Their hearts felt good. In every way, it was a grass roots movement that met the need of the people.

There was rivalry between the various bygdelags in the early days. One of the early leaders became so fanatical about the superiority of his group that it threatened the unity of Norwegians in America. My mother told me that this was often the case. If you weren't from a certain valley, you just didn't count for much among other Norwegians.

229

Unless you've been to Norway and seen the high mountain ranges and valleys, this might seem strange. Even today, despite national television and radio which tends to create uniformity in language, each valley of Norway has its own special way of talking, just like in the United States. Where I grew up, the Hallings and Tronders had difficulty understanding the Sognings. Since the Tronders came from the area of St. Olaf, they were especially sensitive to having "pure blood" among the Norwegians.

The bygdelags were found mostly in Minnesota, Wisconsin, northern Illinois, North and South Dakota. There were also a few in Canada and on the West Coast. There were none organized east of Chicago. Those were interesting days for the newcomers. It's easy to see why so many fellow countrymen settled in the Upper Midwest. There was always someone to welcome them and who would listen eagerly to their bragging about the Old Country which they had left behind.

CHAPTER 99

The Norwegian-American Historical Association

THE IMMIGRANTS TO AMERICA were too busy clearing land, building barns and rearing families to think much about writing their history. It took 100 years before the Norwegian-Americans took that task seriously. Fortunately, a large number of newspapers were published by immigrants and some diaries were available. By the time of the immigration centennial in 1925, a large number of people who knew the oral history were still alive.

The Norwegian-American Historical Association (NAHA) was organized October 6, 1925. Faculty from Luther College in Decorah, Iowa, and St. Olaf College in Northfield, Minnesota, were the key organizers. These were a prestigious group of men who understood modern historical research as influenced by Frederick Jackson Turner and Charles A. Beard. They also understood the dynamics of environment and economics as decisive forces in history.

By the end of 1925, 200 persons had joined the organization. Growth through the years has not been spectacular, but steady. By the end of 1927, there were 842 members. The Great Depression cut into the membership. At the end of 1986, 62 years later, the Association had 1509 members.

I have been a member since 1979 and have been greatly impressed by the wide range and quality of its publications. Two major books a year are released. In 1986, I visited with Prof. Lloyd Hustvedt at the NAHA headquarters in the Rolvaag Memorial Library at St. Olaf College. He has been the Association's Secretary since 1959 and is Editor of its Newsletter. The chief researcher and writer is Prof. Odd S. Lovoll, a native of Norway. He works tirelessly to produce high quality writings. Prof. Lovoll recently wrote a history of Norwegian immigrants in Chicago entitled "A Century of Urban Life: The Norwegians in Chicago Before 1930."

The reason why NAHA can function so well is the solid support of

St. Olaf College. Dr. Sidney A. Rand, former President of St. Olaf and Ambassador to Norway during the Carter administration, was an enthusiastic promoter. He recruited me to membership. One of his goals was a chair in immigration history.

NAHA has had highly competent leadership since its beginnings. Theodore C. Blegen, professor of history and dean of the graduate school in the University of Minnesota, was the Association's managing editor from 1925 to 1960. Prof. Ole Rolvaag, author of "Giants in the Earth" and professor at St. Olaf was one of its founders and served as the first secretary until his death in 1931. J. A. Aasgaard served as president after he retired from the presidency of the Evangelical Lutheran Church (formerly Norwegian Lutheran Church in America) from 1954-1960. The list of leaders includes Ragnvald A. Nestos (1877-1942) of Minot who was governor of North Dakota from 1921-1924. Nestos was an effective recruiter of new members.

The Association was a sponsor of the Norwegian-American Historical Museum in Decorah, Iowa. Begun on the campus of Luther College in 1877, Prof. Knut Gjerset was curator of the museum from 1922 until his death in 1936. This work is carried on today by Vesterheim (Home in the West), an independent museum in Decorah.

The most visible work of NAHA is its publications. In the beginning, volumes were paperbound. But the decision was made to have future works hardbound so that they could be better preserved for future generations. Minot native Jon Wefald's "A Voice of Protest" (1971) launched a series of topical studies. It's a study of "Norwegians in American Politics" from 1890 to 1917 (see chapter 79). The new biographical series has published eight volumes. The series on "Norwegian-American Studies" is the place to look if you want to learn about pioneering in Alaska, Texas, Montana or most any other place Norwegians settled, or about controversial leaders such as Marcus Thrane or the great Telemark skier, Sondre Norheim. Its a goldmine for interesting reading. All of the contributing scholars have donated their research and writing.

A most illustrious volume, "The Promise of America" (1984) by Prof. Lovoll, tells the story of the Norwegian-American people. It's a companion to the exhibit featured in Norway during 1984 and the following year in America. The photographs of pioneer days alone are worth the price of the book. It was first published in Norway and then jointly in America by NAHA and the University of Minnesota Press. It's the best single volume that I've seen to tell the story of Norwegian immigration to America.

Interest in ethnic history is popular in our country now. The "melting pot" didn't completely melt. The Norwegian-American Historical Association deserves the interest and support of all ethnic Norwegians who want good information on their roots. The value of the publications received by members each year far exceeds the cost of membership. For information, write: Norwegian-American Historical Association, St. Olaf College, Northfield, Minnesota 55057.

CHAPTER 100

Geir Botnen —
Norway's World Class Pianist

I F YOU'VE EVER TRAVELLED through the "Vestlands" (Westlands) of Norway, you'll understand why some of the world's most beautiful music has originated there. This was the homeland of Edvard Grieg (1843-1907). When Grieg was asked by Denmark's King Frederick VI who taught him to play the piano, he replied: "I learned from the mountains of Norway."

The sun glistening on the majestic glaciers, the noises of the waterfalls, and the wind blowing through the trees and valleys have inspired many musicians. It's unfortunate that only a few of them have become known outside of Norway.

Geir Botnen (born 1959) is a rising star in the concert halls of Scandinavia. A native of Norheimsund, a small city on a spur of the Hardangerfjord, near Voss and northeast of Bergen, Geir has been captivated by the piano ever since his parents bought one when he was six years old. They arranged lessons for him when he was eight. By 14 they were making weekly trips to Bergen, a two hour drive each way, so he could get advanced instruction. I've driven the road. It's a scenic paradise.

His first teacher was Jan Hovden. At the Bergen Conservatory of Music, Botnen studied with Jiri Hlinka, a famous pianist from Czeckoslovakia who had moved to Norway. Hlinka, who had taken a first at the Tchaikovsky Competition in Moscow, recognized in Botnen a new virtuoso.

Vindication of Hlinka's confidence came in 1982 when Botnen also competed at the Tchaikovsky event and placed high. Near home, he has performed with the Bergen Philharmonic and at Troldhaugen, the home of Edvard Grieg. He has also given recitals in Czeckoslovakia, Denmark and Sweden.

Botnen has been greatly influenced by another outstanding musician from Norheimsund, Geir Tveit (1908-1981), who had studied music in Leipsig, Vienna and Paris, besides his native Norway. By 1938, Tveit had won national recognition for his compositions which were often inspired by the old Norse sagas.

During World War II, when life in Norway was severely restricted by the Nazi occupation, Tveit settled down on the old family farm overlooking the Hardangerfjord. He travelled to many valleys of the area gathering old folk tunes which people sang to him. Afterwards he arranged music for them. He collected over 1000 tunes, but, unfortunately, a fire destroyed most of them.

Fifty tunes of Tveit's collection have survived and Botnen has made an excellent recording in two long play records entitled "Femti Folketonar fra Hardanger" (Fifty Folk Tunes from Hardanger). I have listened to the recordings and it's not difficult to imagine that one is visiting in the Vestlands and being a part of the local festivities.

Botnen has made several trips to the United States to give concerts. In 1984 he spent five weeks on tour as the accompanist for the Gandals Pikekor (a girl's chorus from Gandal in southwestern Norway), travelling from Texas to New York. He returned with them in the summer of 1986. In October 1986, Botnen was the guest soloist with the Minot Symphony Orchestra for the Norsk Høstfest. The Symphony audience was so impressed that Botnen was invited to return for a recital in May 1988.

On this trip to America, he also presented a concert at Augsburg College in Minneapolis and held a master's seminar in piano for faculty and students. While in the Twin Cities, Botnen gave a concert at the Landmark Center in St. Paul which was broadcast live over Minnesota Public Radio. Botnen told me that a string broke on the piano during this performance, the first time this had happened to him. He improvised through the performance so that no one appeared to have noticed it.

Dr. Daniel Hornstein, a professor of music at Minot State University and the Conductor of the Minot's Symphony Orchestra, was highly enthusiastic about Botnen's performance. Hornstein commented that even though Minot has "a remarkable amount and quality of musical activity . . . having the opportunity to hear a world-class artist like Geir

Botnen is unusual even for this community."

Hornstein noted that "Botnen's performance transcended the mere technique of accurately reproducing the written notes and addressed itself directly to the emotional and structural content of the music." I had the same impression as Hornstein that Botnen "was sharing his inner thoughts with the listener through the medium of the music." As witness to the appealing quality of the recital, Hornstein stated that his 12-year-old daughter "was held enraptured for the nearly two-hour recital."

Botnen's appearance in Minot was arranged in part through the encouragement of Dr. Warren Pierson, M.D., a second-cousin. They share a common ancestry in the Botnen family history on the side of Warren's mother. The Botnen's have been a musical legend in Norway for having built the first Hardanger violin, an eight stringed instrument which beautifully reproduces the music of the region.

I had the chance to visit with Geir Botnen before he returned to Norway. He's a delightful conversationalist as well as an exciting musician. He played a couple of Geir Tveit's folk tunes for me. Total animation at the keyboard is the best way to describe him. I don't pretend to be a professional musician or a music scholar, though I've heard some of the world's best perform. There is no doubt in my mind that Hornstein is correct in describing Botnen as "world class." At his Minot recital, he was called back for five curtain calls, once with a standing ovation.

The Minot audience especially enjoyed the four "Lyric Pieces" by Edvard Grieg. The audience was delighted with Grieg's "The Wedding Day at Troldhaugen." It's an example of musical delight plus an unusual amount of artistic emotion. He also played Beethoven's Sonata No. 11 in B flat, opus 22, "Valses nobles et sentimentales" by Maurice Ravel and the very difficult Sonata No. 6, opus 82 by the Russian composer Serge Prokofiev. Most audiences know Prokofiev best through his "Peter and the Wolf." For encores he played "Bustle of Spring" by Sinding and "Prelude from Halbersuite" by Grieg. This is one concert we will not soon forget.

Back in Norway, Botnen lives with his wife, Heidi, and their three small sons, Olav, Tore and Haakon. You can tell from the names of their children that they are great admirers of the Norwegian heritage and the royal family. He teaches piano in the Norheimsund schools and works with groups of students in the nearby schools of the county.

I asked Botnen about his goals. He will make his Oslo debut in September and also expects to play in the Sibelius Hall in Helsinki. His dream is to perform in New York's Carnegie Hall and in the Kennedy Center in Washington, D.C. But he doesn't want to leave his home in Norheimsund to be a full-time traveller. He is deeply appreciative of the quality of life that his home community offers for peaceful reflection that translates into lively music.

Botnen's father, who died in 1971, when Geir was only 12, was an auto mechanic and played the trumpet. His mother, Aslaug, appreciates music, but does not play an instrument. Botnen enjoys servicing automobiles in his spare time. He is also an accomplished trombone player and remembers marching in the Constitution Day parades every May 17. He had to hurry home from Minot to get ready for the 1988 "Syttende Mai" parade.

The amazing thing to me is that Geir Botnen is only 29 years old and has already reached such heights of accomplishment. The world is waiting for musicians of his talent. I hope it doesn't have to wait long before its concert halls ring with sounds of Norway's Vestlands and Botnen's genius.

Geir Botnen.

ORDER FORM

Ship To:

Name _____

Address _____

City_____ State or Province_____ Postal Code_____

QUANTITY

_____ copies of "The Scandinavian World" @ $9.95 per copy

_____ copies of "The Scandinavian Heritage" @ $9.95 per copy

Subtotal _____

ND residents add 5½% sales tax _____

Postage & Handling ($2.00 per book) _____

(Payment should be made in U.S. funds) **Total** _____

Send check or money order to:
North American Heritage Press
P.O. Box 1, Minot, ND 58702

_____

Enjoy another 100 stories and tales of the people, places and history of Scandinavia in "The Scandinavian Heritage" by Arland O. Fiske.

NOW...The Scandinavian Heritage Book. Based on the popular syndicated column by well-known Scandinavian-American author Arland O. Fiske.

The Scandinavian Heritage

Arland O. Fiske

Foreword by Sidney A. [...]

100 interestingly told stories about the people, places, traditions and history of Denmark, Finland, Iceland, Norway and Sweden.

Printed in U.S.A.

ORDER FORM

Ship To:

Name _____

Address _____

City_____ State or
                              Province_____ Postal
                                                   Code_____

QUANTITY

_____ copies of "The Scandinavian World" @ $9.95 per copy

_____ copies of "The Scandinavian Heritage" @ $9.95 per copy

Subtotal _____

ND residents add 5½% sales tax _____

Postage & Handling ($2.00 per book) _____

(Payment should be made in U.S. funds) **Total** _____

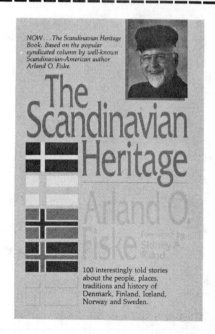
Printed in U.S.A.